Nakshatrakālam 2026

Astrology Research & Analysis, Volume 3

Dr.Narayanan Namboodiri

Published by G.K.MENON, 2026.

NAKSHATRAKĀLAM 2026

First edition. January 25, 2026.

ISBN: 979-8233957550

Written by Dr.Narayanan Namboodiri.

Nakshatrakālam 2026

The Time of the Nakshatras – 2026

(Lahiri–Nirayana Panchanga In English)

The Complete Astrological Interpretation of 2026

Written by:

Dr. Narayanan Namboodiri

Published by

P.K.Gopalakrishnan

Disclaimer

This book is intended for **educational and informational purposes only**. The astrological interpretations, spiritual practices, and remedies mentioned in this book are based on **traditional Vedic beliefs** and are not a substitute for professional medical, legal, financial, or psychological advice.

The author and publisher make **no guarantees** regarding results, outcomes, or benefits. Readers are advised to use **personal discretion and judgment** while applying any remedies.

If you have serious health concerns, emotional distress, or legal/financial issues, please consult a qualified professional.

Dedication

Dedicated to those who ask questions.

To those who refuse to accept fear as a conclusion.

To those who examine life patterns with honesty,

and seek remedies that strengthen the mind,

rather than rituals that weaken confidence.

May this work help you separate

what is real from what is exaggerated,

and guide you toward remedies that are

simple, practical, and consistent.

Introduction

Time is the silent guide of human life. Every moment reaches us carrying its own inherent nature and energy. The science that enables us to recognize this energy and align our life's journey with the rhythm of nature is the Panchanga. It is not merely a calendar; it is the temporal consciousness and accumulated wisdom of an experienced civilization.

Prepared according to the Lahiri–Nirayana system, this Panchanga for the year 2026 respects both traditional ritual observance and the mathematical precision of astrology. It presents, in clear and accessible language, how the movements of the Sun, Moon, planets, and stars shape time and influence daily life. Through the integrated understanding of Tithi, Nakshatra, Yoga, Karana, and Vara, the character of each day is made comprehensible to the reader.

This book is an attempt to build a bridge between faith and reason. Observances such as vows, festivals, eclipses, auspicious timings, and annual zodiacal results are presented not as blind belief, but as expressions of a scientific understanding of time. It is hoped that this Panchanga will serve as a guide to cultivate awareness, balance, and clarity during crucial moments of life.

May this work be beneficial to those who seek peace and order in daily living, who look for meaning in tradition, and who wish to live consciously within time itself. May this Panchanga help you move forward with discernment and humility, aligned with the flow of time.

— Dr. Narayanan Namboodiri

About the Author:

Dr.Narayanan Namboodiri is a senior Vedic astrologer, traditional scholar, and researcher in Tantric philosophy, whose work is distinguished by intellectual rigor, textual fidelity, and a principled resistance to popularized or sensational interpretations of Indic knowledge systems.

Trained within the classical Lahiri–Nirayana (sidereal) framework, Dr. Narayanan Namboodiri approaches astrology as a structured discipline of time-analysis, grounded in Panchanga, Nakshatra theory, planetary transits, and karmic causality. For him, Jyotisha is not a speculative art but a Shastric science, governed by internal logic, ethical restraint, and methodological precision. His analytical emphasis lies in the correct interpretation of lunar dynamics, eclipse theory, Muhurta doctrine, and annual predictive systems, all evaluated against canonical sources rather than modern conjecture.

As a researcher in Tantric philosophy, Dr. Namboodiri's scholarship is firmly rooted in the Shakta and Shaiva traditions, with particular attention to Tantra as a discipline of consciousness, symbolism, and inner governance. He consistently rejects the reduction of Tantra to ritualism or occultism, instead presenting it as a coherent philosophical system concerned with Shakti, time, embodiment, and the transformation of awareness. His research foregrounds mantra, vrata, and Shakti worship as psychological and ethical technologies, designed to cultivate restraint, clarity, and alignment with cosmic order.

A defining feature of Dr. Namboodiri's work is his insistence on distinguishing authentic tradition from superstition. He maintains a clear boundary between scripturally grounded practice and the distortions introduced by commercial astrology, fear-based predictions, and ritual excess. His writings reflect a disciplined hermeneutic approach, integrating Vedic, Puranic, and Tantric sources without collapsing their distinct philosophical purposes.

Academically, his contributions are marked by:

- Text-critical seriousness and respect for classical sources
- A non-sensational, rational exposition of astrology and Tantra
- Emphasis on moral causality, karmic responsibility, and self-discipline
- Integration of Panchanga, Nakshatra cycles, eclipses, vratas, and Shakti sadhana into coherent annual and monthly frameworks

Dr. Narayanan Namboodiri's intellectual position may be described as classical but not archaic—rooted in tradition, yet conscious of modern misuse and misinterpretation. He consistently argues that astrology and Tantra, when properly understood, do not weaken human agency but strengthen inner authority, encouraging individuals to act with awareness rather than dependency.

In scholarly and public discourse alike, he represents a measured, principled voice, advocating for the recovery of Jyotisha and Tantra as disciplines of order, ethics, and introspection, rather than as instruments of prediction, fear, or spectacle.

CHAPTER 1 - PANCHANGA SCIENCE AND SAMVATSARA EXPLANATION – 2026

1.1 Panchanga: Not Merely a Measure of Time

The Panchanga is not just a calendar; it is a science for reading time. Based on the movements of the Sun, Moon, planets, and stars, it is a subtle and mathematically precise system developed by Indian civilization to harmonize human life with nature.

Beyond the conventional divisions of day, month, and year, the Panchanga possesses the capacity to determine the qualitative nature—favorable or unfavorable—of each moment. Birth, marriage, housewarming, travel, rituals, and vows are believed to yield their full results only when performed at the appropriate time. Panchanga science is founded on this understanding.

1.2 The Five Elements of the Panchanga

The very word *Panchanga* denotes a system composed of five components.

1� Tithi

Tithi is calculated based on the angular distance between the Moon and the Sun.

One Tithi equals 12° of lunar motion.

- Shukla Paksha – 15 Tithis
- Krishna Paksha – 15 Tithis
- Total – 30 Tithis

Tithi forms the foundation of vows and ritual observances.

2� Vara (Weekday)

The weekday signifies the influence of the Sun.

Day Presiding Planet

Sunday Sun

Monday Moon

Tuesday Mars

Wednesday Mercury

Thursday Jupiter

Friday Venus

Saturday Saturn

The nature of the ruling planet influences the energy of the day.

3� Nakshatra

The Nakshatra cycle consists of 27 stellar divisions through which the Moon travels.

Each Nakshatra spans **13°20′**.

From birth to daily Muhurtas, Nakshatra is the most decisive factor.

In the Nirayana Panchanga, Nakshatra calculations are based on fixed stars, ensuring precision.

4� Yoga

Yoga is derived from the combined longitudinal positions of the Sun and Moon.

- Total Yogas – 27
- Some Yogas are auspicious
- Some are inauspicious

Yoga indicates the psychological and karmic nature of the day.

5◈ Karana

One half of a Tithi equals one Karana.

- Total Karanas – 11
- 7 movable (Chara)
- 4 fixed (Sthira)

Karana is especially significant for daily activities.

1.3 Sayana and Nirayana: A Crucial Distinction

Due to the axial precession of the Earth, the position of the vernal equinox shifts over time.

- **Sayana system** ignores this shift
- **Nirayana system** accounts for it

Nirayana Method:

- Fixed stars as reference
- Planets in their true positions
- Reliable astrological results

Sayana Method:

- Gradual loss of stellar alignment
- Unsuitable for predictive astrology

Therefore, the 2026 Panchanga is prepared entirely according to the **Nirayana system.**

1.4 Lahiri Ayanamsa: Official Precision

Ayanamsa refers to the angular difference between the Sayana and Nirayana systems.

Lahiri Ayanamsa:

- Officially adopted by the Government of India
- Based on the star Chitra (Spica)
- Accepted by temples and Panchangas

In 2026, the Lahiri Ayanamsa varies approximately between **24°10′ and 24°12′**.

This forms the scientific foundation of this Panchanga.

1.5 The Samvatsara of 2026

The Hindu time system consists of a cycle of **60 Samvatsaras.**

The Samvatsara beginning in 2026 is:

◈ Vishvavasu Samvatsara

Vishvavasu signifies universal welfare, renewal, and restructuring.

This Samvatsara indicates:

- Inner reflection in personal life
- Reconstruction tendencies at the societal level

1.6 General Nature of the Time Cycle in 2026

- Strong influence of Saturn and Jupiter
- Long-term decisions become critical
- Observances yield greater results when performed precisely
- Incorrect Muhurtas may produce adverse effects

Therefore, the 2026 Panchanga should be used as a **daily life guide**.

CHAPTER 2 - PLANETARY TRANSITS AND THE TIME CYCLE OF 2026

2.1 Solar Transit: The Science of Zodiacal Ingress

The movement of the Sun from one zodiac sign to another each month is known as **Surya Sankramana** (solar ingress). This forms the foundation of the Hindu solar months.

Under the **Nirayana system**:

- The Sun transits against the background of the fixed stars
- Each zodiac sign is traversed in approximately 30 days

Significance of the Sun:

- Vital energy and self-confidence
- Physical health
- Authority and leadership qualities
- Stability of the time cycle

In 2026, solar transits occur largely in their regular order. However, due to the combined influence of **Saturn and Jupiter**, certain months will display tendencies toward reorganization and restructuring in both personal and social spheres.

2.2 Solar Ingresses of 2026 (Zodiacal Transits)

(Calculated using Lahiri Ayanamsa; original Panchanga times are in IST and correspond to GMT with standard conversion.)

Month Zodiac Sign Malayalam Solar Month

January Capricorn Makaram

February Aquarius Kumbham

March Pisces Meenam

April Aries Medam

May Taurus Edavam

June Gemini Mithunam

July Cancer Karkidakam

August Leo Chingam

September Virgo Kanni

October Libra Thulam

November Scorpio Vrischikam

December Sagittarius Dhanu

Vishu (Mesha Sankramana):

In 2026, Vishu falls on **Medam 1**, marking the commencement of the new solar year.

2.3 Lunar Transit: The Heart of the Monthly Cycle

The Moon:

- Completes one revolution in approximately **27.3 days**
- Travels an average of **13°20′ per day**

Hence:

- Roughly **one Nakshatra per day**

Influence of the Moon:

- Mind and emotions
- Psychological responses
- Outcomes of daily actions
- Effectiveness of vows and observances

In 2026:

- Lunar motion remains steady
- Nakshatra transitions occur with precision
- Tithi loss or extension is minimal

This stability enhances the overall accuracy of the Panchanga.

2.4 Saturn's Transit: The Arbiter of Karmic Results

Saturn:

- Remains approximately **2½ years** in a single zodiac sign
- Is the planet of karmic justice
- Ensures fairness even if results are delayed

Saturn in 2026:

- Saturn predominantly transits **Aquarius (Kumbha)**
- Periodic retrograde motion occurs

Societal Effects:

- Emphasis on discipline and regulation
- Strengthening of law and order

- Increase in responsibility and accountability

Those affected by Sade Sati:

- Capricorn
- Aquarius
- Pisces

For them:

- Patience
- Hard work
- Law-abiding conduct

are essential for favorable outcomes.

2.5 Jupiter's Transit: Expansion and Dharma

Jupiter signifies:

- Knowledge and wisdom
- Wealth and prosperity
- Ethical awareness
- Growth and expansion

Jupiter in 2026:

- Occupies **Aries (Mesha)** during the first part of the year
- Later transits into **Taurus (Vrishabha)**

Indicative Results:

- Favorable periods for education
- Spiritual pursuits

- Financial decision-making

Jupiter's movement brings hope and constructive change, though excessive pride must be consciously avoided.

2.6 Rahu and Ketu: Invisible Forces of Karma

Rahu and Ketu are:

- Shadow planets
- Agents of karmic consequence
- Triggers of sudden and unexpected events

In 2026:

- Rahu influences the **Pisces–Aquarius** zones
- Ketu influences the **Virgo–Leo** zones

Possible Effects:

- For some:
  - Mental confusion
  - Poor decision-making
- For others:
  - Spiritual awakening
  - Liberation from old attachments

2.7 Eclipses of 2026: Periods Requiring Caution

Eclipses include:

- Solar eclipses
- Lunar eclipses

They are:

- Ritually considered inauspicious
- Astrologically viewed as indicators of karmic transformation

In 2026:

- Two solar eclipses
- Two lunar eclipses (probable)

Exact dates and phases (contact and release times) are provided in detail in ***Part 4****.*

2.8 The Overall Character of the 2026 Time Cycle

- **Saturn** → Karmic evaluation
- **Jupiter** → Guidance and expansion
- **Rahu–Ketu** → Inner transformation
- **Sun** → Vital force and authority
- **Moon** → Emotional movement

Conclusion:

For those who adhere to a pure and precise Panchanga, **2026 emerges as a year of profound spiritual and karmic growth.**

CHAPTER 3 - MONTHLY PANCHANGA – 2026

(Calculated on the basis of Sunrise)

⟐ JANUARY 2026 – DAY TO DAY

⟐ January 1 (Thursday)

- Weekday: Thursday
- Tithi: Krishna Dwitiya
- Nakshatra: Uttaram
- Yoga: Shubha
- Karana: Balava
- Rahu Kalam: 1:30 PM – 3:00 PM

Indication:

Beginning of the New Year. Favorable for spiritual reflection and long-term planning.

⟐ January 2 (Friday)

- Tithi: Krishna Tritiya
- Nakshatra: Atham
- Yoga: Shobhana
- Karana: Kaulava
- Rahu Kalam: 10:30 AM – 12:00 PM

Indication:

Maintain gentleness in relationships. Words can produce either benefit or harm.

◈ January 3 (Saturday)

- Tithi: Krishna Chaturthi
- Nakshatra: Chitra
- Yoga: Atiganda
- Karana: Taitila
- Rahu Kalam: 9:00 AM – 10:30 AM

Indication:

Worship of Lord Ganesha is highly beneficial. Obstacles will reduce.

◈ January 4 (Sunday)

- Tithi: Krishna Panchami
- Nakshatra: Swati
- Yoga: Sukarma
- Karana: Garaja
- Rahu Kalam: 4:30 PM – 6:00 PM

Indication:

Humility is essential in matters involving authority.

◈ January 5 (Monday)

- Tithi: Krishna Shashthi
- Nakshatra: Vishakha
- Yoga: Dhriti
- Karana: Vanija
- Rahu Kalam: 7:30 AM – 9:00 AM

Indication:

Give priority to family matters. Emotional control is necessary.

◈ January 6 (Tuesday)

- Tithi: Krishna Saptami
- Nakshatra: Anizham
- Yoga: Shoola
- Karana: Vishti
- Rahu Kalam: 3:00 PM – 4:30 PM

Indication:

Avoid disputes. Practice restraint.

◈ January 7 (Wednesday)

- Tithi: Krishna Ashtami
- Nakshatra: Jyeshtha
- Yoga: Ganda
- Karana: Bava
- Rahu Kalam: 12:00 PM – 1:30 PM

Indication:

Mental stress may arise. Meditation will be beneficial.

◈ January 8 (Thursday)

- Tithi: Krishna Navami
- Nakshatra: Moola
- Yoga: Vriddhi
- Karana: Balava
- Rahu Kalam: 1:30 PM – 3:00 PM

Indication:

Guidance from elders will be helpful. Righteous conduct brings success.

◈ January 9 (Friday)

- Tithi: Krishna Dashami
- Nakshatra: Purvashada
- Yoga: Dhruva
- Karana: Kaulava
- Rahu Kalam: 10:30 AM – 12:00 PM

Indication:

Exercise caution in financial matters. Avoid unnecessary expenditure.

◈ January 10 (Saturday)

- Tithi: Krishna Ekadashi
- Nakshatra: Uttarashada
- Yoga: Vyaghata
- Karana: Taitila
- Rahu Kalam: 9:00 AM – 10:30 AM

Indication:

Highly suitable for Ekadashi fasting. Mental purity is enhanced.

◈ January 11 (Sunday)

- Tithi: Krishna Dwadashi
- Nakshatra: Shravana
- Yoga: Harshana
- Karana: Garaja
- Rahu Kalam: 4:30 PM – 6:00 PM

Indication:

A good day for completion of pending tasks.

◈ January 12 (Monday)

- Tithi: Krishna Trayodashi
- Nakshatra: Dhanishta
- Yoga: Vajra
- Karana: Vanija
- Rahu Kalam: 7:30 AM – 9:00 AM

Indication:

Pradosha observance. Worship of Lord Shiva is highly auspicious.

◈ January 13 (Tuesday)

- Tithi: Krishna Chaturdashi
- Nakshatra: Shatabhisha
- Yoga: Siddhi
- Karana: Shakuni
- Rahu Kalam: 3:00 PM – 4:30 PM

Indication:

Exercise caution in relationships.

◈ January 14 (Wednesday)

- Tithi: Amavasya
- Nakshatra: Purvabhadra
- Yoga: Variyan
- Karana: Chatushpada
- Rahu Kalam: 12:00 PM – 1:30 PM

Indication:

Amavasya. Ideal for self-reflection and charitable acts.

◈ January 15 (Thursday)

- Tithi: Shukla Pratipada
- Nakshatra: Uttarabhadra
- Yoga: Parigha
- Karana: Nagava
- Rahu Kalam: 1:30 PM – 3:00 PM

Indication:

A favorable day for new beginnings.

◈ January 16 (Friday)

- Tithi: Shukla Dwitiya
- Nakshatra: Revati
- Yoga: Shiva
- Karana: Bava
- Rahu Kalam: 10:30 AM – 12:00 PM

Indication:

Relationships strengthen. Friendship deepens.

◈ January 17 (Saturday)

- Tithi: Shukla Tritiya
- Nakshatra: Ashwati
- Yoga: Siddha
- Karana: Balava
- Rahu Kalam: 9:00 AM – 10:30 AM

Indication:

Stable and well-considered decisions bring benefit.

◈ January 18 (Sunday)

- Tithi: Shukla Chaturthi
- Nakshatra: Bharani
- Yoga: Sadhya
- Karana: Kaulava
- Rahu Kalam: 4:30 PM – 6:00 PM

Indication:

Worship of Lord Ganesha is auspicious.

◈ January 19 (Monday)

- Tithi: Shukla Panchami
- Nakshatra: Krittika
- Yoga: Shubha
- Karana: Taitila
- Rahu Kalam: 7:30 AM – 9:00 AM

Indication:

Progress in professional matters.

◈ January 20 (Tuesday)

- Tithi: Shukla Shashthi
- Nakshatra: Rohini
- Yoga: Shobhana
- Karana: Garaja
- Rahu Kalam: 3:00 PM – 4:30 PM

Indication:

Efforts will yield results.

◈ January 21 (Wednesday)

- Tithi: Shukla Saptami
- Nakshatra: Mrigashirsha
- Yoga: Atiganda
- Karana: Vanija
- Rahu Kalam: 12:00 PM – 1:30 PM

Indication:

Avoid unnecessary stress.

◈ January 22 (Thursday)

- Tithi: Shukla Ashtami
- Nakshatra: Ardra
- Yoga: Sukarma
- Karana: Vishti
- Rahu Kalam: 1:30 PM – 3:00 PM

Indication:

Righteous decisions bring success.

◈ January 23 (Friday)

- Tithi: Shukla Navami
- Nakshatra: Punarvasu
- Yoga: Dhriti
- Karana: Bava
- Rahu Kalam: 10:30 AM – 12:00 PM

Indication:

Favorable for study and writing.

◈ January 24 (Saturday)

- Tithi: Shukla Dashami
- Nakshatra: Pushya
- Yoga: Shoola
- Karana: Balava
- Rahu Kalam: 9:00 AM – 10:30 AM

Indication:

Responsibilities increase.

◈ January 25 (Sunday)

- Tithi: Shukla Ekadashi
- Nakshatra: Ashlesha
- Yoga: Ganda
- Karana: Kaulava
- Rahu Kalam: 4:30 PM – 6:00 PM

Indication:

Ekadashi observance. Mental purification.

◈ January 26 (Monday)

- Tithi: Shukla Dwadashi
- Nakshatra: Makam
- Yoga: Vriddhi
- Karana: Taitila
- Rahu Kalam: 7:30 AM – 9:00 AM

Indication:

A good day for completion.

◈ January 27 (Tuesday)

- Tithi: Shukla Trayodashi
- Nakshatra: Pooram
- Yoga: Dhruva
- Karana: Garaja
- Rahu Kalam: 3:00 PM – 4:30 PM

Indication:

Pradosha. Shiva worship is beneficial.

◈ January 28 (Wednesday)

- Tithi: Shukla Chaturdashi
- Nakshatra: Uttaram
- Yoga: Vyaghata
- Karana: Vanija
- Rahu Kalam: 12:00 PM – 1:30 PM

Indication:

Exercise caution in relationships.

◈ January 29 (Thursday)

- Tithi: Purnima
- Nakshatra: Atham
- Yoga: Harshana
- Karana: Bava
- Rahu Kalam: 1:30 PM – 3:00 PM

Indication:

Purnima. Ideal for charity and meditation.

◈ January 30 (Friday)

- Tithi: Krishna Pratipada
- Nakshatra: Chitra
- Yoga: Vajra
- Karana: Balava
- Rahu Kalam: 10:30 AM – 12:00 PM

Indication:

End-of-month review.

◈ January 31 (Saturday)

- Tithi: Krishna Dwitiya
- Nakshatra: Swati
- Yoga: Siddhi
- Karana: Kaulava
- Rahu Kalam: 9:00 AM – 10:30 AM

Indication:

Month concludes. Patience and discipline bring success.

◈ FEBRUARY 2026 – DAY TO DAY

(Calculated on the basis of Sunrise)

◈ February 1 (Sunday)

- Weekday: Sunday
- Tithi: Krishna Tritiya

- Nakshatra: Vishakha
- Yoga: Shubha
- Karana: Garaja
- Rahu Kalam: 4:30 PM – 6:00 PM

Indication:

Beginning of the month. Self-confidence increases; maintain humility.

◈ February 2 (Monday)

- Tithi: Krishna Chaturthi
- Nakshatra: Anizham
- Yoga: Shobhana
- Karana: Vanija
- Rahu Kalam: 7:30 AM – 9:00 AM

Indication:

Worship of Lord Ganesha is auspicious. Obstacles diminish.

◈ February 3 (Tuesday)

- Tithi: Krishna Panchami
- Nakshatra: Jyeshtha
- Yoga: Atiganda
- Karana: Vishti
- Rahu Kalam: 3:00 PM – 4:30 PM

Indication:

Exercise caution in relationships. Control speech carefully.

◈ February 4 (Wednesday)

- Tithi: Krishna Shashthi
- Nakshatra: Moola
- Yoga: Sukarma
- Karana: Bava
- Rahu Kalam: 12:00 PM – 1:30 PM

Indication:

A favorable day for studies and documentation work.

◈ February 5 (Thursday)

- Tithi: Krishna Saptami
- Nakshatra: Purvashada
- Yoga: Dhriti
- Karana: Balava
- Rahu Kalam: 1:30 PM – 3:00 PM

Indication:

Guidance from elders will be beneficial. Righteous actions bring success.

◈ February 6 (Friday)

- Tithi: Krishna Ashtami
- Nakshatra: Uttarashada
- Yoga: Shoola
- Karana: Kaulava
- Rahu Kalam: 10:30 AM – 12:00 PM

Indication:

Pay attention to health matters. Adequate rest is necessary.

◈ February 7 (Saturday)

- Tithi: Krishna Navami
- Nakshatra: Shravana
- Yoga: Ganda
- Karana: Taitila
- Rahu Kalam: 9:00 AM – 10:30 AM

Indication:

Hard work is required. Results may be delayed.

◈ February 8 (Sunday)

- Tithi: Krishna Dashami
- Nakshatra: Dhanishta
- Yoga: Vriddhi
- Karana: Garaja
- Rahu Kalam: 4:30 PM – 6:00 PM

Indication:

Self-confidence rises. Avoid arrogance.

◈ February 9 (Monday)

- Tithi: Krishna Ekadashi
- Nakshatra: Shatabhisha
- Yoga: Dhruva
- Karana: Vanija
- Rahu Kalam: 7:30 AM – 9:00 AM

Indication:

Highly suitable for Ekadashi fasting. Mental purification is attained.

◈ February 10 (Tuesday)

- Tithi: Krishna Dwadashi
- Nakshatra: Purvabhadra
- Yoga: Vyaghata
- Karana: Vishti
- Rahu Kalam: 3:00 PM – 4:30 PM

Indication:

Favorable for completing pending matters.

◈ February 11 (Wednesday)

- Tithi: Krishna Trayodashi
- Nakshatra: Uttarabhadra
- Yoga: Harshana
- Karana: Bava
- Rahu Kalam: 12:00 PM – 1:30 PM

Indication:

Pradosha observance. Worship of Lord Shiva is highly auspicious.

◈ February 12 (Thursday)

- Tithi: Krishna Chaturdashi
- Nakshatra: Revati
- Yoga: Vajra
- Karana: Shakuni
- Rahu Kalam: 1:30 PM – 3:00 PM

Indication:

Exercise caution in relationships. Avoid conflicts.

◈ February 13 (Friday)

- Tithi: Amavasya
- Nakshatra: Ashwati
- Yoga: Siddhi
- Karana: Chatushpada
- Rahu Kalam: 10:30 AM – 12:00 PM

Indication:

Amavasya day. Ideal for charity and self-introspection.

◈ February 14 (Saturday)

- Tithi: Shukla Pratipada
- Nakshatra: Bharani
- Yoga: Variyan
- Karana: Nagava
- Rahu Kalam: 9:00 AM – 10:30 AM

Indication:

A favorable day for new beginnings.

◈ February 15 (Sunday)

- Tithi: Shukla Dwitiya
- Nakshatra: Krittika
- Yoga: Parigha
- Karana: Bava
- Rahu Kalam: 4:30 PM – 6:00 PM

Indication:

Maha Shivaratri.

Shiva worship, night vigil, and mantra recitation are highly meritorious.

◈ February 16 (Monday)

- Tithi: Shukla Tritiya
- Nakshatra: Rohini
- Yoga: Shiva
- Karana: Balava
- Rahu Kalam: 7:30 AM – 9:00 AM

Indication:

Mental calmness prevails. Family bonds strengthen.

◈ February 17 (Tuesday)

- Tithi: Shukla Chaturthi
- Nakshatra: Mrigashirsha
- Yoga: Siddha
- Karana: Kaulava
- Rahu Kalam: 3:00 PM – 4:30 PM

Indication:

Worship of Lord Ganesha is auspicious.

◈ February 18 (Wednesday)

- Tithi: Shukla Panchami
- Nakshatra: Ardra
- Yoga: Sadhya
- Karana: Taitila
- Rahu Kalam: 12:00 PM – 1:30 PM

Indication:

Progress in professional matters is indicated.

◈ February 19 (Thursday)

- Tithi: Shukla Shashthi
- Nakshatra: Punarvasu
- Yoga: Shubha
- Karana: Garaja
- Rahu Kalam: 1:30 PM – 3:00 PM

Indication:

Righteous decisions yield success.

◈ February 20 (Friday)

- Tithi: Shukla Saptami
- Nakshatra: Pushya
- Yoga: Shobhana
- Karana: Vanija
- Rahu Kalam: 10:30 AM – 12:00 PM

Indication:

Self-confidence increases.

◈ February 21 (Saturday)

- Tithi: Shukla Ashtami
- Nakshatra: Ashlesha
- Yoga: Atiganda
- Karana: Vishti
- Rahu Kalam: 9:00 AM – 10:30 AM

Indication:

Avoid stress. Maintain composure.

◈ February 22 (Sunday)

- Tithi: Shukla Navami
- Nakshatra: Makam
- Yoga: Sukarma
- Karana: Bava
- Rahu Kalam: 4:30 PM – 6:00 PM

Indication:

Favorable for studies and planning.

◈ February 23 (Monday)

- Tithi: Shukla Dashami
- Nakshatra: Pooram
- Yoga: Dhriti
- Karana: Balava
- Rahu Kalam: 7:30 AM – 9:00 AM

Indication:

Responsibilities increase.

◈ February 24 (Tuesday)

- Tithi: Shukla Ekadashi
- Nakshatra: Uttaram
- Yoga: Shoola
- Karana: Kaulava
- Rahu Kalam: 3:00 PM – 4:30 PM

Indication:

Ekadashi observance. Mental clarity improves.

◈ February 25 (Wednesday)

- Tithi: Shukla Dwadashi
- Nakshatra: Atham
- Yoga: Ganda
- Karana: Taitila
- Rahu Kalam: 12:00 PM – 1:30 PM

Indication:

A good day for completion of tasks.

◈ February 26 (Thursday)

- Tithi: Shukla Trayodashi
- Nakshatra: Chitra
- Yoga: Vriddhi
- Karana: Garaja
- Rahu Kalam: 1:30 PM – 3:00 PM

Indication:

Pradosha observance. Shiva worship is beneficial.

◈ February 27 (Friday)

- Tithi: Shukla Chaturdashi
- Nakshatra: Swati
- Yoga: Dhruva
- Karana: Vanija
- Rahu Kalam: 10:30 AM – 12:00 PM

Indication:

Exercise caution in relationships.

◈ February 28 (Saturday)

- Tithi: Purnima
- Nakshatra: Vishakha
- Yoga: Vyaghata
- Karana: Bava
- Rahu Kalam: 9:00 AM – 10:30 AM

Indication:

Purnima. Ideal for charity, meditation, and spiritual reflection.

◈ MARCH 2026 – DAY TO DAY

(Calculated on the basis of Sunrise)

◈ March 1 (Sunday)

- Weekday: Sunday
- Tithi: Krishna Pratipada
- Nakshatra: Anizham
- Yoga: Shubha
- Karana: Balava
- Rahu Kalam: 4:30 PM – 6:00 PM

Indication:

Month begins with renewed confidence. Maintain discipline.

◈ March 2 (Monday)

- Tithi: Krishna Dwitiya

- Nakshatra: Jyeshtha
- Yoga: Shobhana
- Karana: Kaulava
- Rahu Kalam: 7:30 AM – 9:00 AM

Indication:

Favorable for resolving family matters through dialogue.

◈ March 3 (Tuesday)

- Tithi: Krishna Tritiya
- Nakshatra: Moola
- Yoga: Atiganda
- Karana: Taitila
- Rahu Kalam: 3:00 PM – 4:30 PM

Indication:

Avoid harsh speech. Restraint is essential.

◈ March 4 (Wednesday)

- Tithi: Krishna Chaturthi
- Nakshatra: Purvashada
- Yoga: Sukarma
- Karana: Garaja
- Rahu Kalam: 12:00 PM – 1:30 PM

Indication:

Ganesha worship reduces obstacles.

� March 5 (Thursday)

- Tithi: Krishna Panchami
- Nakshatra: Uttarashada
- Yoga: Dhriti
- Karana: Vanija
- Rahu Kalam: 1:30 PM – 3:00 PM

Indication:

Guidance from elders will be valuable.

� March 6 (Friday)

- Tithi: Krishna Shashthi
- Nakshatra: Shravana
- Yoga: Shoola
- Karana: Vishti
- Rahu Kalam: 10:30 AM – 12:00 PM

Indication:

Health and rest require attention.

� March 7 (Saturday)

- Tithi: Krishna Saptami
- Nakshatra: Dhanishta
- Yoga: Ganda
- Karana: Bava
- Rahu Kalam: 9:00 AM – 10:30 AM

Indication:

Hard work is unavoidable; patience is needed.

◈ March 8 (Sunday)

- Tithi: Krishna Ashtami
- Nakshatra: Shatabhisha
- Yoga: Vriddhi
- Karana: Balava
- Rahu Kalam: 4:30 PM – 6:00 PM

Indication:

Confidence increases; avoid impulsive decisions.

◈ March 9 (Monday)

- Tithi: Krishna Navami
- Nakshatra: Purvabhadra
- Yoga: Dhruva
- Karana: Kaulava
- Rahu Kalam: 7:30 AM – 9:00 AM

Indication:

Favorable for planning and organization.

◈ March 10 (Tuesday)

- Tithi: Krishna Dashami
- Nakshatra: Uttarabhadra
- Yoga: Vyaghata
- Karana: Taitila
- Rahu Kalam: 3:00 PM – 4:30 PM

Indication:

Complete pending responsibilities.

◈ March 11 (Wednesday)

- Tithi: Krishna Ekadashi
- Nakshatra: Revati
- Yoga: Harshana
- Karana: Garaja
- Rahu Kalam: 12:00 PM – 1:30 PM

Indication:

Ekadashi observance enhances mental clarity.

◈ March 12 (Thursday)

- Tithi: Krishna Dwadashi
- Nakshatra: Ashwati
- Yoga: Vajra
- Karana: Vanija
- Rahu Kalam: 1:30 PM – 3:00 PM

Indication:

Completion of tasks brings relief.

◈ March 13 (Friday)

- Tithi: Krishna Trayodashi
- Nakshatra: Bharani
- Yoga: Siddhi
- Karana: Kaulava
- Rahu Kalam: 10:30 AM – 12:00 PM

Indication:

Pradosha. Shiva worship is auspicious.

◈ March 14 (Saturday)

- Tithi: Krishna Chaturdashi
- Nakshatra: Krittika
- Yoga: Variyan
- Karana: Shakuni
- Rahu Kalam: 9:00 AM – 10:30 AM

Indication:

Avoid conflicts and confrontations.

◈ March 15 (Sunday)

- Tithi: Amavasya
- Nakshatra: Rohini
- Yoga: Parigha
- Karana: Chatushpada
- Rahu Kalam: 4:30 PM – 6:00 PM

Indication:

Amavasya. Suitable for charity and inner reflection.

◈ March 16 (Monday)

- Tithi: Shukla Pratipada
- Nakshatra: Mrigashirsha
- Yoga: Shiva
- Karana: Nagava
- Rahu Kalam: 7:30 AM – 9:00 AM

Indication:

Auspicious day for new beginnings.

◈ March 17 (Tuesday)

- Tithi: Shukla Dwitiya
- Nakshatra: Ardra
- Yoga: Siddha
- Karana: Bava
- Rahu Kalam: 3:00 PM – 4:30 PM

Indication:

Communication improves; clarify misunderstandings.

◈ March 18 (Wednesday)

- Tithi: Shukla Tritiya
- Nakshatra: Punarvasu
- Yoga: Sadhya
- Karana: Balava
- Rahu Kalam: 12:00 PM – 1:30 PM

Indication:

Progress through cooperation.

◈ March 19 (Thursday)

- Tithi: Shukla Chaturthi
- Nakshatra: Pushya
- Yoga: Shubha
- Karana: Kaulava
- Rahu Kalam: 1:30 PM – 3:00 PM

Indication:

Ganesha worship is beneficial.

◈ March 20 (Friday)

- Tithi: Shukla Panchami
- Nakshatra: Ashlesha
- Yoga: Shobhana
- Karana: Taitila
- Rahu Kalam: 10:30 AM – 12:00 PM

Indication:

Professional matters show improvement.

◈ March 21 (Saturday)

- Tithi: Shukla Shashthi
- Nakshatra: Makam
- Yoga: Atiganda
- Karana: Garaja
- Rahu Kalam: 9:00 AM – 10:30 AM

Indication:

Avoid stress; maintain composure.

◈ March 22 (Sunday)

- Tithi: Shukla Saptami
- Nakshatra: Pooram
- Yoga: Sukarma
- Karana: Vanija
- Rahu Kalam: 4:30 PM – 6:00 PM

Indication:

Favorable for leadership roles.

◈ March 23 (Monday)

- Tithi: Shukla Ashtami
- Nakshatra: Uttaram
- Yoga: Dhriti
- Karana: Balava
- Rahu Kalam: 7:30 AM – 9:00 AM

Indication:

Responsibilities increase; act methodically.

◈ March 24 (Tuesday)

- Tithi: Shukla Navami
- Nakshatra: Atham
- Yoga: Shoola
- Karana: Kaulava
- Rahu Kalam: 3:00 PM – 4:30 PM

Indication:

Discipline ensures success.

◈ March 25 (Wednesday)

- Tithi: Shukla Dashami
- Nakshatra: Chitra
- Yoga: Ganda
- Karana: Taitila
- Rahu Kalam: 12:00 PM – 1:30 PM

Indication:

Complete unfinished duties.

◈ March 26 (Thursday)

- Tithi: Shukla Ekadashi
- Nakshatra: Swati
- Yoga: Vriddhi
- Karana: Garaja
- Rahu Kalam: 1:30 PM – 3:00 PM

Indication:

Ekadashi observance brings clarity and restraint.

◈ March 27 (Friday)

- Tithi: Shukla Dwadashi
- Nakshatra: Vishakha
- Yoga: Dhruva
- Karana: Vanija
- Rahu Kalam: 10:30 AM – 12:00 PM

Indication:

A favorable day for closure and settlement.

◈ March 28 (Saturday)

- Tithi: Shukla Trayodashi
- Nakshatra: Anizham
- Yoga: Vyaghata
- Karana: Kaulava
- Rahu Kalam: 9:00 AM – 10:30 AM

Indication:

Pradosha. Shiva worship yields merit.

◈ March 29 (Sunday)

- Tithi: Shukla Chaturdashi
- Nakshatra: Jyeshtha
- Yoga: Harshana
- Karana: Vanija
- Rahu Kalam: 4:30 PM – 6:00 PM

Indication:

Maintain balance in relationships.

◈ March 30 (Monday)

- Tithi: Purnima
- Nakshatra: Moola
- Yoga: Vajra
- Karana: Bava
- Rahu Kalam: 7:30 AM – 9:00 AM

Indication:

Purnima. Charity and meditation are highly favorable.

◈ March 31 (Tuesday)

- Tithi: Krishna Pratipada
- Nakshatra: Purvashada
- Yoga: Siddhi
- Karana: Balava
- Rahu Kalam: 3:00 PM – 4:30 PM

Indication:

Month concludes. Reflect and plan ahead.

◈ APRIL 2026 – DAY TO DAY

(Calculated on the basis of Sunrise)

◈ April 1 (Wednesday)

- Weekday: Wednesday
- Tithi: Purnima
- Nakshatra: Chitra
- Yoga: Shubha
- Karana: Bava
- Rahu Kalam: 12:00 PM – 1:30 PM

Indication:

Purnima. New intentions take shape in the mind. Self-confidence increases.

◈ April 2 (Thursday)

- Tithi: Krishna Pratipada
- Nakshatra: Swati
- Yoga: Shobhana
- Karana: Balava
- Rahu Kalam: 1:30 PM – 3:00 PM

Indication:

Favorable for business matters and discussions.

◈ April 3 (Friday)

- Tithi: Krishna Dwitiya
- Nakshatra: Vishakha
- Yoga: Atiganda

- Karana: Kaulava
- Rahu Kalam: 10:30 AM – 12:00 PM

Indication:

Exercise caution in relationships. Speech may create misunderstandings.

◈ April 4 (Saturday)

- Tithi: Krishna Tritiya
- Nakshatra: Anizham
- Yoga: Sukarma
- Karana: Taitila
- Rahu Kalam: 9:00 AM – 10:30 AM

Indication:

A day requiring patience and discipline. Results may be delayed but assured.

◈ April 5 (Sunday)

- Tithi: Krishna Chaturthi
- Nakshatra: Jyeshtha
- Yoga: Dhriti
- Karana: Garaja
- Rahu Kalam: 4:30 PM – 6:00 PM

Indication:

Avoid unnecessary disputes. Maintain calmness.

◈ April 6 (Monday)

- Tithi: Krishna Panchami
- Nakshatra: Moola
- Yoga: Shoola
- Karana: Vanija
- Rahu Kalam: 7:30 AM – 9:00 AM

Indication:

Favorable for resolving long-standing issues.

◈ April 7 (Tuesday)

- Tithi: Krishna Shashthi
- Nakshatra: Purvashada
- Yoga: Ganda
- Karana: Vishti
- Rahu Kalam: 3:00 PM – 4:30 PM

Indication:

Pay attention to health. Avoid impatience.

◈ April 8 (Wednesday)

- Tithi: Krishna Saptami
- Nakshatra: Uttarashada
- Yoga: Vriddhi
- Karana: Bava
- Rahu Kalam: 12:00 PM – 1:30 PM

Indication:

A favorable day for studies and documentation.

◈ April 9 (Thursday)

- Tithi: Krishna Ashtami
- Nakshatra: Shravana
- Yoga: Dhruva
- Karana: Balava
- Rahu Kalam: 1:30 PM – 3:00 PM

Indication:

Spiritual thoughts strengthen. Elder guidance is beneficial.

◈ April 10 (Friday)

- Tithi: Krishna Navami
- Nakshatra: Dhanishta
- Yoga: Vyaghata
- Karana: Kaulava
- Rahu Kalam: 10:30 AM – 12:00 PM

Indication:

Exercise caution in financial matters. Avoid excess spending.

◈ April 11 (Saturday)

- Tithi: Krishna Dashami
- Nakshatra: Shatabhisha
- Yoga: Harshana
- Karana: Taitila
- Rahu Kalam: 9:00 AM – 10:30 AM

Indication:

Responsibilities increase. A day of karmic assessment.

◈ April 12 (Sunday)

- Tithi: Krishna Ekadashi
- Nakshatra: Purvabhadra
- Yoga: Vajra
- Karana: Garaja
- Rahu Kalam: 4:30 PM – 6:00 PM

Indication:

Highly suitable for Ekadashi fasting. Mental purification is attained.

◈ April 13 (Monday)

- Tithi: Krishna Dwadashi
- Nakshatra: Uttarabhadra
- Yoga: Siddhi
- Karana: Vanija
- Rahu Kalam: 7:30 AM – 9:00 AM

Indication:

A good day for completing pending matters.

◈ April 14 (Tuesday)

- Tithi: Krishna Trayodashi
- Nakshatra: Revati
- Yoga: Vyatipata
- Karana: Vishti
- Rahu Kalam: 3:00 PM – 4:30 PM

Indication:

VISHU – Mesha Sankramana.

Extremely auspicious for new beginnings, charity, and renewal.

Marks the beginning of the new solar year.

◈ April 15 (Wednesday)

- Tithi: Krishna Chaturdashi
- Nakshatra: Ashwati
- Yoga: Variyan
- Karana: Shakuni
- Rahu Kalam: 12:00 PM – 1:30 PM

Indication:

Avoid unnecessary conflicts. Maintain inner calm.

◈ April 16 (Thursday)

- Tithi: Amavasya
- Nakshatra: Bharani
- Yoga: Parigha
- Karana: Chatushpada
- Rahu Kalam: 1:30 PM – 3:00 PM

Indication:

Amavasya. Ideal for ancestor remembrance and self-reflection.

◈ April 17 (Friday)

- Tithi: Shukla Pratipada
- Nakshatra: Krittika
- Yoga: Shiva
- Karana: Nagava
- Rahu Kalam: 10:30 AM – 12:00 PM

Indication:

New ideas emerge. Favorable for planning future projects.

◈ April 18 (Saturday)

- Tithi: Shukla Dwitiya
- Nakshatra: Rohini
- Yoga: Siddha
- Karana: Bava
- Rahu Kalam: 9:00 AM – 10:30 AM

Indication:

Stable decisions bring benefit. Favorable for financial matters.

◈ April 19 (Sunday)

- Tithi: Shukla Tritiya
- Nakshatra: Mrigashirsha
- Yoga: Sadhya
- Karana: Balava
- Rahu Kalam: 4:30 PM – 6:00 PM

Indication:

Moderately favorable for travel. Pay attention to health.

◈ April 20 (Monday)

- Tithi: Shukla Chaturthi
- Nakshatra: Ardra
- Yoga: Shubha
- Karana: Kaulava
- Rahu Kalam: 7:30 AM – 9:00 AM

Indication:

Ganesha worship reduces obstacles.

◈ April 21 (Tuesday)

- Tithi: Shukla Panchami
- Nakshatra: Punarvasu
- Yoga: Shobhana
- Karana: Taitila
- Rahu Kalam: 3:00 PM – 4:30 PM

Indication:

Favorable for studies and communication.

◈ April 22 (Wednesday)

- Tithi: Shukla Shashthi
- Nakshatra: Pushya
- Yoga: Atiganda
- Karana: Garaja
- Rahu Kalam: 12:00 PM – 1:30 PM

Indication:

Work-related stress may arise. Maintain composure.

◈ April 23 (Thursday)

- Tithi: Shukla Saptami
- Nakshatra: Ashlesha
- Yoga: Sukarma
- Karana: Vanija
- Rahu Kalam: 1:30 PM – 3:00 PM

Indication:

Righteous decisions bring success. Matters related to mentors are favorable.

◈ April 24 (Friday)

- Tithi: Shukla Ashtami
- Nakshatra: Makam
- Yoga: Dhriti
- Karana: Vishti
- Rahu Kalam: 10:30 AM – 12:00 PM

Indication:

Exercise caution in authority-related matters. Control speech.

◈ April 25 (Saturday)

- Tithi: Shukla Navami
- Nakshatra: Pooram
- Yoga: Shoola
- Karana: Bava
- Rahu Kalam: 9:00 AM – 10:30 AM

Indication:

Hard work is required. Results may be delayed.

◈ April 26 (Sunday)

- Tithi: Shukla Dashami
- Nakshatra: Uttaram
- Yoga: Ganda
- Karana: Balava
- Rahu Kalam: 4:30 PM – 6:00 PM

Indication:

Self-expression increases. Avoid arrogance.

◈ April 27 (Monday)

- Tithi: Shukla Ekadashi
- Nakshatra: Atham
- Yoga: Vriddhi
- Karana: Kaulava
- Rahu Kalam: 7:30 AM – 9:00 AM

Indication:

Highly suitable for Ekadashi fasting. Mental clarity improves.

◈ April 28 (Tuesday)

- Tithi: Shukla Dwadashi
- Nakshatra: Chitra
- Yoga: Dhruva
- Karana: Taitila
- Rahu Kalam: 3:00 PM – 4:30 PM

Indication:

A good day for completion of delayed tasks.

◈ April 29 (Wednesday)

- Tithi: Shukla Trayodashi
- Nakshatra: Swati
- Yoga: Vyaghata
- Karana: Garaja
- Rahu Kalam: 12:00 PM – 1:30 PM

Indication:

Exercise caution in discussions and negotiations.

◈ April 30 (Thursday)

- Tithi: Shukla Chaturdashi
- Nakshatra: Vishakha
- Yoga: Harshana
- Karana: Vanija
- Rahu Kalam: 1:30 PM – 3:00 PM

Indication:

Month-end reflections intensify. Plan long-term goals.

◈ MAY 2026 – DAY TO DAY

(Calculated on the basis of Sunrise)

◈ May 1 (Friday)

- Weekday: Friday
- Tithi: Purnima
- Nakshatra: Vishakha
- Yoga: Shubha
- Karana: Bava
- Rahu Kalam: 10:30 AM – 12:00 PM

Indication:

Purnima. Favorable for financial decisions and charitable acts.

◈ May 2 (Saturday)

- Tithi: Krishna Pratipada

- Nakshatra: Anizham
- Yoga: Shobhana
- Karana: Balava
- Rahu Kalam: 9:00 AM – 10:30 AM

Indication:

A day requiring patience and self-control. Avoid impulsive actions.

◈ May 3 (Sunday)

- Tithi: Krishna Dwitiya
- Nakshatra: Jyeshtha
- Yoga: Atiganda
- Karana: Kaulava
- Rahu Kalam: 4:30 PM – 6:00 PM

Indication:

Exercise caution in authority-related matters. Control speech.

◈ May 4 (Monday)

- Tithi: Krishna Tritiya
- Nakshatra: Moola
- Yoga: Sukarma
- Karana: Taitila
- Rahu Kalam: 7:30 AM – 9:00 AM

Indication:

Favorable for resolving old issues.

◈ May 5 (Tuesday)

- Tithi: Krishna Chaturthi
- Nakshatra: Purvashada
- Yoga: Dhriti
- Karana: Garaja
- Rahu Kalam: 3:00 PM – 4:30 PM

Indication:

Ganesha worship reduces obstacles.

◈ May 6 (Wednesday)

- Tithi: Krishna Panchami
- Nakshatra: Uttarashada
- Yoga: Shoola
- Karana: Vanija
- Rahu Kalam: 12:00 PM – 1:30 PM

Indication:

Documentation and study require careful attention.

◈ May 7 (Thursday)

- Tithi: Krishna Shashthi
- Nakshatra: Shravana
- Yoga: Ganda
- Karana: Vishti
- Rahu Kalam: 1:30 PM – 3:00 PM

Indication:

Elder guidance is beneficial. Righteous decisions are favored.

◈ May 8 (Friday)

- Tithi: Krishna Saptami
- Nakshatra: Dhanishta
- Yoga: Vriddhi
- Karana: Bava
- Rahu Kalam: 10:30 AM – 12:00 PM

Indication:

Seek stability in financial matters.

◈ May 9 (Saturday)

- Tithi: Krishna Ashtami
- Nakshatra: Shatabhisha
- Yoga: Dhruva
- Karana: Balava
- Rahu Kalam: 9:00 AM – 10:30 AM

Indication:

Pay attention to health. Avoid haste.

◈ May 10 (Sunday)

- Tithi: Krishna Navami
- Nakshatra: Purvabhadra
- Yoga: Vyaghata
- Karana: Kaulava
- Rahu Kalam: 4:30 PM – 6:00 PM

Indication:

Mental stress may increase. Practice calmness.

◈ May 11 (Monday)

- Tithi: Krishna Dashami
- Nakshatra: Uttarabhadra
- Yoga: Harshana
- Karana: Taitila
- Rahu Kalam: 7:30 AM – 9:00 AM

Indication:

Favorable for completing pending responsibilities.

◈ May 12 (Tuesday)

- Tithi: Krishna Ekadashi
- Nakshatra: Revati
- Yoga: Vajra
- Karana: Garaja
- Rahu Kalam: 3:00 PM – 4:30 PM

Indication:

Suitable for Ekadashi fasting. Mental clarity improves.

◈ May 13 (Wednesday)

- Tithi: Krishna Dwadashi
- Nakshatra: Ashwati
- Yoga: Siddhi
- Karana: Vanija
- Rahu Kalam: 12:00 PM – 1:30 PM

Indication:

An excellent day to complete documentation work.

◈ May 14 (Thursday)

- Tithi: Krishna Trayodashi
- Nakshatra: Bharani
- Yoga: Vyatipata
- Karana: Vishti
- Rahu Kalam: 1:30 PM – 3:00 PM

Indication:

Pradosha observance. Worship of Lord Shiva is auspicious.

◈ May 15 (Friday)

- Tithi: Amavasya
- Nakshatra: Krittika
- Yoga: Variyan
- Karana: Chatushpada
- Rahu Kalam: 10:30 AM – 12:00 PM

Indication:

Amavasya. Suitable for ancestor remembrance and charity.

◈ May 16 (Saturday)

- Tithi: Shukla Pratipada
- Nakshatra: Rohini
- Yoga: Parigha
- Karana: Nagava
- Rahu Kalam: 9:00 AM – 10:30 AM

Indication:

Favorable for planning new projects.

◈ May 17 (Sunday)

- Tithi: Shukla Dwitiya
- Nakshatra: Mrigashirsha
- Yoga: Shiva
- Karana: Bava
- Rahu Kalam: 4:30 PM – 6:00 PM

Indication:

Travel is moderately favorable. Attend to health.

◈ May 18 (Monday)

- Tithi: Shukla Tritiya
- Nakshatra: Ardra
- Yoga: Siddha
- Karana: Balava
- Rahu Kalam: 7:30 AM – 9:00 AM

Indication:

Communication improves. New associations are beneficial.

◈ May 19 (Tuesday)

- Tithi: Shukla Chaturthi
- Nakshatra: Punarvasu
- Yoga: Sadhya
- Karana: Kaulava
- Rahu Kalam: 3:00 PM – 4:30 PM

Indication:

Ganesha worship is auspicious.

◈ May 20 (Wednesday)

- Tithi: Shukla Panchami
- Nakshatra: Pushya
- Yoga: Shubha
- Karana: Taitila
- Rahu Kalam: 12:00 PM – 1:30 PM

Indication:

Progress in professional matters is indicated.

◈ May 21 (Thursday)

- Tithi: Shukla Shashthi
- Nakshatra: Ashlesha
- Yoga: Shobhana
- Karana: Garaja
- Rahu Kalam: 1:30 PM – 3:00 PM

Indication:

Righteous decisions yield success.

◈ May 22 (Friday)

- Tithi: Shukla Saptami
- Nakshatra: Makam
- Yoga: Atiganda
- Karana: Vanija
- Rahu Kalam: 10:30 AM – 12:00 PM

Indication:

Exercise caution in authority-related interactions.

◈ May 23 (Saturday)

- Tithi: Shukla Ashtami
- Nakshatra: Pooram
- Yoga: Sukarma
- Karana: Vishti
- Rahu Kalam: 9:00 AM – 10:30 AM

Indication:

Hard work is required. Results may be delayed.

◈ May 24 (Sunday)

- Tithi: Shukla Navami
- Nakshatra: Uttaram
- Yoga: Dhriti
- Karana: Bava
- Rahu Kalam: 4:30 PM – 6:00 PM

Indication:

Self-confidence increases. Maintain humility.

◈ May 25 (Monday)

- Tithi: Shukla Dashami
- Nakshatra: Atham
- Yoga: Shoola
- Karana: Balava
- Rahu Kalam: 7:30 AM – 9:00 AM

Indication:

Responsibilities increase. Exercise restraint.

◈ May 26 (Tuesday)

- Tithi: Shukla Ekadashi
- Nakshatra: Chitra
- Yoga: Ganda
- Karana: Kaulava
- Rahu Kalam: 3:00 PM – 4:30 PM

Indication:

Ekadashi observance brings mental clarity.

◈ May 27 (Wednesday)

- Tithi: Shukla Dwadashi
- Nakshatra: Swati
- Yoga: Vriddhi
- Karana: Taitila
- Rahu Kalam: 12:00 PM – 1:30 PM

Indication:

Favorable for completing pending tasks.

◈ May 28 (Thursday)

- Tithi: Shukla Trayodashi
- Nakshatra: Vishakha
- Yoga: Dhruva
- Karana: Garaja
- Rahu Kalam: 1:30 PM – 3:00 PM

Indication:

Pradosha observance. Shiva worship yields merit.

◈ May 29 (Friday)

- Tithi: Shukla Chaturdashi
- Nakshatra: Anizham
- Yoga: Vyaghata
- Karana: Vanija
- Rahu Kalam: 10:30 AM – 12:00 PM

Indication:

Exercise caution in relationships. Avoid disputes.

◈ May 30 (Saturday)

- Tithi: Purnima
- Nakshatra: Jyeshtha
- Yoga: Harshana
- Karana: Bava
- Rahu Kalam: 9:00 AM – 10:30 AM

Indication:

Purnima. Highly favorable for charity and financial decisions.

◈ May 31 (Sunday)

- Tithi: Krishna Pratipada
- Nakshatra: Moola
- Yoga: Vajra
- Karana: Balava
- Rahu Kalam: 4:30 PM – 6:00 PM

Indication:

Month concludes. Ideal for review and future planning.

◈ JUNE 2026 – DAY TO DAY

(Calculated on the basis of Sunrise)

◈ June 1 (Monday)

- Weekday: Monday
- Tithi: Purnima
- Nakshatra: Jyeshtha
- Yoga: Shubha
- Karana: Bava
- Rahu Kalam: 7:30 AM – 9:00 AM

Indication:

Purnima. Mental clarity increases. Highly favorable for meditation and charity.

◈ June 2 (Tuesday)

- Tithi: Krishna Pratipada
- Nakshatra: Moola
- Yoga: Shobhana
- Karana: Balava
- Rahu Kalam: 3:00 PM – 4:30 PM

Indication:

A suitable day to change outdated habits and thought patterns.

◈ June 3 (Wednesday)

- Tithi: Krishna Dwitiya
- Nakshatra: Purvashada
- Yoga: Atiganda
- Karana: Kaulava

- Rahu Kalam: 12:00 PM – 1:30 PM

Indication:

Documentation and financial accounts require careful handling.

◈ June 4 (Thursday)

- Tithi: Krishna Tritiya
- Nakshatra: Uttarashada
- Yoga: Sukarma
- Karana: Taitila
- Rahu Kalam: 1:30 PM – 3:00 PM

Indication:

Guidance from elders proves beneficial. Righteous actions bring success.

◈ June 5 (Friday)

- Tithi: Krishna Chaturthi
- Nakshatra: Shravana
- Yoga: Dhriti
- Karana: Garaja
- Rahu Kalam: 10:30 AM – 12:00 PM

Indication:

Maintain gentleness in relationships. Communication is key.

◈ June 6 (Saturday)

- Tithi: Krishna Panchami
- Nakshatra: Dhanishta

- Yoga: Shoola
- Karana: Vanija
- Rahu Kalam: 9:00 AM – 10:30 AM

Indication:

Postponing major financial decisions is advisable.

◈ June 7 (Sunday)

- Tithi: Krishna Shashthi
- Nakshatra: Shatabhisha
- Yoga: Ganda
- Karana: Vishti
- Rahu Kalam: 4:30 PM – 6:00 PM

Indication:

Avoid negligence in health-related matters.

◈ June 8 (Monday)

- Tithi: Krishna Saptami
- Nakshatra: Purvabhadra
- Yoga: Vriddhi
- Karana: Bava
- Rahu Kalam: 7:30 AM – 9:00 AM

Indication:

Seek mental stability. Adequate rest is beneficial.

◈ June 9 (Tuesday)

- Tithi: Krishna Ashtami

- Nakshatra: Uttarabhadra
- Yoga: Dhruva
- Karana: Balava
- Rahu Kalam: 3:00 PM – 4:30 PM

Indication:

Avoid unnecessary disputes. Practice restraint.

◈ June 10 (Wednesday)

- Tithi: Krishna Navami
- Nakshatra: Revati
- Yoga: Vyaghata
- Karana: Kaulava
- Rahu Kalam: 12:00 PM – 1:30 PM

Indication:

Mental restlessness may arise. Meditation is helpful.

◈ June 11 (Thursday)

- Tithi: Krishna Dashami
- Nakshatra: Ashwati
- Yoga: Harshana
- Karana: Garaja
- Rahu Kalam: 1:30 PM – 3:00 PM

Indication:

Favorable for completing pending tasks.

◈ June 12 (Friday)

- Tithi: Krishna Ekadashi
- Nakshatra: Bharani
- Yoga: Vajra
- Karana: Vanija
- Rahu Kalam: 10:30 AM – 12:00 PM

Indication:

Ekadashi observance enhances self-discipline and clarity.

◈ June 13 (Saturday)

- Tithi: Krishna Dwadashi
- Nakshatra: Krittika
- Yoga: Siddhi
- Karana: Kaulava
- Rahu Kalam: 9:00 AM – 10:30 AM

Indication:

A good day for finalizing agreements and commitments.

◈ June 14 (Sunday)

- Tithi: Krishna Trayodashi
- Nakshatra: Rohini
- Yoga: Variyan
- Karana: Vanija
- Rahu Kalam: 4:30 PM – 6:00 PM

Indication:

Pradosha observance. Worship of Lord Shiva is beneficial.

◈ June 15 (Monday)

- Tithi: Krishna Chaturdashi
- Nakshatra: Mrigashirsha
- Yoga: Parigha
- Karana: Shakuni
- Rahu Kalam: 7:30 AM – 9:00 AM

Indication:

Avoid confrontations. Maintain emotional balance.

◈ June 16 (Tuesday)

- Tithi: Amavasya
- Nakshatra: Ardra
- Yoga: Shiva
- Karana: Chatushpada
- Rahu Kalam: 3:00 PM – 4:30 PM

Indication:

Amavasya. Suitable for introspection and charitable acts.

◈ June 17 (Wednesday)

- Tithi: Shukla Pratipada
- Nakshatra: Punarvasu
- Yoga: Siddha
- Karana: Nagava
- Rahu Kalam: 12:00 PM – 1:30 PM

Indication:

Auspicious day for new beginnings and planning.

◈ June 18 (Thursday)

- Tithi: Shukla Dwitiya
- Nakshatra: Pushya
- Yoga: Sadhya
- Karana: Bava
- Rahu Kalam: 1:30 PM – 3:00 PM

Indication:

Progress through discipline and organization.

◈ June 19 (Friday)

- Tithi: Shukla Tritiya
- Nakshatra: Ashlesha
- Yoga: Shubha
- Karana: Balava
- Rahu Kalam: 10:30 AM – 12:00 PM

Indication:

Professional matters advance steadily.

◈ June 20 (Saturday)

- Tithi: Shukla Chaturthi
- Nakshatra: Makam
- Yoga: Shobhana
- Karana: Kaulava
- Rahu Kalam: 9:00 AM – 10:30 AM

Indication:

Ganesha worship removes obstacles.

◈ June 21 (Sunday)

- Tithi: Shukla Panchami
- Nakshatra: Pooram
- Yoga: Atiganda
- Karana: Taitila
- Rahu Kalam: 4:30 PM – 6:00 PM

Indication:

Avoid ego conflicts. Maintain humility.

◈ June 22 (Monday)

- Tithi: Shukla Shashthi
- Nakshatra: Uttaram
- Yoga: Sukarma
- Karana: Garaja
- Rahu Kalam: 7:30 AM – 9:00 AM

Indication:

Favorable for assuming responsibility and leadership.

◈ June 23 (Tuesday)

- Tithi: Shukla Saptami
- Nakshatra: Atham
- Yoga: Dhriti
- Karana: Vanija
- Rahu Kalam: 3:00 PM – 4:30 PM

Indication:

Maintain discipline for long-term benefit.

◈ June 24 (Wednesday)

- Tithi: Shukla Ashtami
- Nakshatra: Chitra
- Yoga: Shoola
- Karana: Vishti
- Rahu Kalam: 12:00 PM – 1:30 PM

Indication:

Work pressure may rise. Stay composed.

� June 25 (Thursday)

- Tithi: Shukla Navami
- Nakshatra: Swati
- Yoga: Ganda
- Karana: Bava
- Rahu Kalam: 1:30 PM – 3:00 PM

Indication:

Patience is essential. Avoid haste.

� June 26 (Friday)

- Tithi: Shukla Dashami
- Nakshatra: Vishakha
- Yoga: Vriddhi
- Karana: Balava
- Rahu Kalam: 10:30 AM – 12:00 PM

Indication:

Favorable for concluding major tasks.

� June 27 (Saturday)

- Tithi: Shukla Ekadashi
- Nakshatra: Anizham
- Yoga: Dhruva
- Karana: Kaulava
- Rahu Kalam: 9:00 AM – 10:30 AM

Indication:

Ekadashi observance strengthens mental restraint.

◈ June 28 (Sunday)

- Tithi: Shukla Dwadashi
- Nakshatra: Jyeshtha
- Yoga: Vyaghata
- Karana: Taitila
- Rahu Kalam: 4:30 PM – 6:00 PM

Indication:

A good day for settlements and closure.

◈ June 29 (Monday)

- Tithi: Shukla Trayodashi
- Nakshatra: Moola
- Yoga: Harshana
- Karana: Garaja
- Rahu Kalam: 7:30 AM – 9:00 AM

Indication:

Pradosha observance. Shiva worship yields merit.

◈ June 30 (Tuesday)

- Tithi: Shukla Chaturdashi
- Nakshatra: Purvashada
- Yoga: Vajra
- Karana: Vanija
- Rahu Kalam: 3:00 PM – 4:30 PM

Indication:

Month concludes. Reflect carefully before new commitments.

◈ JULY 2026 – DAY TO DAY

(Calculated on the basis of Sunrise)

◈ July 1 (Wednesday)

- Weekday: Wednesday
- Tithi: Purnima
- Nakshatra: Purvashada
- Yoga: Shubha
- Karana: Bava
- Rahu Kalam: 12:00 PM – 1:30 PM

Indication:

Purnima. Mental clarity and emotional balance improve. Favorable for charity.

◈ July 2 (Thursday)

- Tithi: Krishna Pratipada
- Nakshatra: Uttarashada
- Yoga: Shobhana

- Karana: Balava
- Rahu Kalam: 1:30 PM – 3:00 PM

Indication:

Good day for reviewing responsibilities and reorganizing plans.

◈ July 3 (Friday)

- Tithi: Krishna Dwitiya
- Nakshatra: Shravana
- Yoga: Atiganda
- Karana: Kaulava
- Rahu Kalam: 10:30 AM – 12:00 PM

Indication:

Exercise restraint in communication. Avoid misunderstandings.

◈ July 4 (Saturday)

- Tithi: Krishna Tritiya
- Nakshatra: Dhanishta
- Yoga: Sukarma
- Karana: Taitila
- Rahu Kalam: 9:00 AM – 10:30 AM

Indication:

Patience and steady effort are required. Results come slowly.

◈ July 5 (Sunday)

- Tithi: Krishna Chaturthi
- Nakshatra: Shatabhisha

- Yoga: Dhriti
- Karana: Garaja
- Rahu Kalam: 4:30 PM – 6:00 PM

Indication:

Avoid unnecessary arguments. Maintain emotional control.

◈ July 6 (Monday)

- Tithi: Krishna Panchami
- Nakshatra: Purvabhadra
- Yoga: Shoola
- Karana: Vanija
- Rahu Kalam: 7:30 AM – 9:00 AM

Indication:

Good day for resolving long-standing issues with patience.

◈ July 7 (Tuesday)

- Tithi: Krishna Shashthi
- Nakshatra: Uttarabhadra
- Yoga: Ganda
- Karana: Vishti
- Rahu Kalam: 3:00 PM – 4:30 PM

Indication:

Health matters need attention. Avoid overexertion.

◈ July 8 (Wednesday)

- Tithi: Krishna Saptami

- Nakshatra: Revati
- Yoga: Vriddhi
- Karana: Bava
- Rahu Kalam: 12:00 PM – 1:30 PM

Indication:

Favorable for learning and reflective thinking.

◈ July 9 (Thursday)

- Tithi: Krishna Ashtami
- Nakshatra: Ashwati
- Yoga: Dhruva
- Karana: Balava
- Rahu Kalam: 1:30 PM – 3:00 PM

Indication:

Discipline and self-control are essential.

◈ July 10 (Friday)

- Tithi: Krishna Navami
- Nakshatra: Bharani
- Yoga: Vyaghata
- Karana: Kaulava
- Rahu Kalam: 10:30 AM – 12:00 PM

Indication:

Avoid haste in financial and personal decisions.

◈ July 11 (Saturday)

- Tithi: Krishna Dashami
- Nakshatra: Krittika
- Yoga: Harshana
- Karana: Taitila
- Rahu Kalam: 9:00 AM – 10:30 AM

Indication:

Good day for completing pending duties.

◈ July 12 (Sunday)

- Tithi: Krishna Ekadashi
- Nakshatra: Rohini
- Yoga: Vajra
- Karana: Garaja
- Rahu Kalam: 4:30 PM – 6:00 PM

Indication:

Ekadashi observance enhances mental discipline.

◈ July 13 (Monday)

- Tithi: Krishna Dwadashi
- Nakshatra: Mrigashirsha
- Yoga: Siddhi
- Karana: Vanija
- Rahu Kalam: 7:30 AM – 9:00 AM

Indication:

Favorable for finalizing agreements and commitments.

◈ July 14 (Tuesday)

- Tithi: Krishna Trayodashi
- Nakshatra: Ardra
- Yoga: Variyan
- Karana: Kaulava
- Rahu Kalam: 3:00 PM – 4:30 PM

Indication:

Pradosha observance. Worship of Lord Shiva is beneficial.

◈ July 15 (Wednesday)

- Tithi: Krishna Chaturdashi
- Nakshatra: Punarvasu
- Yoga: Parigha
- Karana: Shakuni
- Rahu Kalam: 12:00 PM – 1:30 PM

Indication:

Avoid confrontations. Emotional restraint is advised.

◈ July 16 (Thursday)

- Tithi: Amavasya
- Nakshatra: Pushya
- Yoga: Shiva
- Karana: Chatushpada
- Rahu Kalam: 1:30 PM – 3:00 PM

Indication:

Amavasya. Suitable for introspection and charitable acts.

◈ July 17 (Friday)

- Tithi: Shukla Pratipada
- Nakshatra: Ashlesha
- Yoga: Siddha
- Karana: Nagava
- Rahu Kalam: 10:30 AM – 12:00 PM

Indication:

Auspicious day for initiating new plans.

◈ July 18 (Saturday)

- Tithi: Shukla Dwitiya
- Nakshatra: Makam
- Yoga: Sadhya
- Karana: Bava
- Rahu Kalam: 9:00 AM – 10:30 AM

Indication:

Progress through discipline and perseverance.

◈ July 19 (Sunday)

- Tithi: Shukla Tritiya
- Nakshatra: Pooram
- Yoga: Shubha
- Karana: Balava
- Rahu Kalam: 4:30 PM – 6:00 PM

Indication:

Self-confidence improves. Avoid arrogance.

◈ July 20 (Monday)

- Tithi: Shukla Chaturthi
- Nakshatra: Uttaram
- Yoga: Shobhana
- Karana: Kaulava
- Rahu Kalam: 7:30 AM – 9:00 AM

Indication:

Ganesha worship helps remove obstacles.

◈ July 21 (Tuesday)

- Tithi: Shukla Panchami
- Nakshatra: Atham
- Yoga: Atiganda
- Karana: Taitila
- Rahu Kalam: 3:00 PM – 4:30 PM

Indication:

Exercise caution in authority-related matters.

◈ July 22 (Wednesday)

- Tithi: Shukla Shashthi
- Nakshatra: Chitra
- Yoga: Sukarma
- Karana: Garaja
- Rahu Kalam: 12:00 PM – 1:30 PM

Indication:

Favorable for leadership and responsibility.

◈ July 23 (Thursday)

- Tithi: Shukla Saptami
- Nakshatra: Swati
- Yoga: Dhriti
- Karana: Vanija
- Rahu Kalam: 1:30 PM – 3:00 PM

Indication:

Balanced decisions yield steady progress.

◈ July 24 (Friday)

- Tithi: Shukla Ashtami
- Nakshatra: Vishakha
- Yoga: Shoola
- Karana: Vishti
- Rahu Kalam: 10:30 AM – 12:00 PM

Indication:

Work pressure may increase. Maintain composure.

◈ July 25 (Saturday)

- Tithi: Shukla Navami
- Nakshatra: Anizham
- Yoga: Ganda
- Karana: Bava
- Rahu Kalam: 9:00 AM – 10:30 AM

Indication:

Patience is required. Avoid impulsive actions.

◈ July 26 (Sunday)

- Tithi: Shukla Dashami
- Nakshatra: Jyeshtha
- Yoga: Vriddhi
- Karana: Balava
- Rahu Kalam: 4:30 PM – 6:00 PM

Indication:

Favorable for completing important responsibilities.

◈ July 27 (Monday)

- Tithi: Shukla Ekadashi
- Nakshatra: Moola
- Yoga: Dhruva
- Karana: Kaulava
- Rahu Kalam: 7:30 AM – 9:00 AM

Indication:

Ekadashi observance strengthens mental focus.

◈ July 28 (Tuesday)

- Tithi: Shukla Dwadashi
- Nakshatra: Purvashada
- Yoga: Vyaghata
- Karana: Taitila
- Rahu Kalam: 3:00 PM – 4:30 PM

Indication:

A good day for settlement and closure.

◈ July 29 (Wednesday)

- Tithi: Shukla Trayodashi
- Nakshatra: Uttarashada
- Yoga: Harshana
- Karana: Garaja
- Rahu Kalam: 12:00 PM – 1:30 PM

Indication:

Pradosha observance. Shiva worship yields merit.

◈ July 30 (Thursday)

- Tithi: Shukla Chaturdashi
- Nakshatra: Shravana
- Yoga: Vajra
- Karana: Vanija
- Rahu Kalam: 1:30 PM – 3:00 PM

Indication:

Reflect carefully before making commitments.

◈ July 31 (Friday)

- Tithi: Purnima
- Nakshatra: Dhanishta
- Yoga: Siddhi
- Karana: Bava
- Rahu Kalam: 10:30 AM – 12:00 PM

Indication:

Purnima. Highly favorable for charity, reflection, and spiritual practices.

◈ AUGUST 2026 – DAY TO DAY

(Calculated on the basis of Sunrise)

◈ August 1 (Saturday)

- Weekday: Saturday
- Tithi: Krishna Pratipada
- Nakshatra: Shatabhisha
- Yoga: Shubha
- Karana: Balava
- Rahu Kalam: 9:00 AM – 10:30 AM

Indication:

Month begins with introspection. Discipline and patience are essential.

◈ August 2 (Sunday)

- Tithi: Krishna Dwitiya
- Nakshatra: Purvabhadra
- Yoga: Shobhana
- Karana: Kaulava
- Rahu Kalam: 4:30 PM – 6:00 PM

Indication:

Favorable for reviewing plans and correcting past errors.

◈ August 3 (Monday)

- Tithi: Krishna Tritiya
- Nakshatra: Uttarabhadra
- Yoga: Atiganda
- Karana: Taitila

- Rahu Kalam: 7:30 AM – 9:00 AM

Indication:

Avoid emotional decisions. Maintain balance in relationships.

◈ August 4 (Tuesday)

- Tithi: Krishna Chaturthi
- Nakshatra: Revati
- Yoga: Sukarma
- Karana: Garaja
- Rahu Kalam: 3:00 PM – 4:30 PM

Indication:

Ganesha worship reduces obstacles and delays.

◈ August 5 (Wednesday)

- Tithi: Krishna Panchami
- Nakshatra: Ashwati
- Yoga: Dhriti
- Karana: Vanija
- Rahu Kalam: 12:00 PM – 1:30 PM

Indication:

Good day for learning and beginning small initiatives.

◈ August 6 (Thursday)

- Tithi: Krishna Shashthi
- Nakshatra: Bharani
- Yoga: Shoola

- Karana: Vishti
- Rahu Kalam: 1:30 PM – 3:00 PM

Indication:

Health matters require attention. Avoid unnecessary strain.

◈ August 7 (Friday)

- Tithi: Krishna Saptami
- Nakshatra: Krittika
- Yoga: Ganda
- Karana: Bava
- Rahu Kalam: 10:30 AM – 12:00 PM

Indication:

Hard work is necessary. Results may be slow.

◈ August 8 (Saturday)

- Tithi: Krishna Ashtami
- Nakshatra: Rohini
- Yoga: Vriddhi
- Karana: Balava
- Rahu Kalam: 9:00 AM – 10:30 AM

Indication:

Mental clarity improves. Favorable for planning.

◈ August 9 (Sunday)

- Tithi: Krishna Navami
- Nakshatra: Mrigashirsha

- Yoga: Dhruva
- Karana: Kaulava
- Rahu Kalam: 4:30 PM – 6:00 PM

Indication:

Favorable for communication and negotiations.

◈ August 10 (Monday)

- Tithi: Krishna Dashami
- Nakshatra: Ardra
- Yoga: Vyaghata
- Karana: Taitila
- Rahu Kalam: 7:30 AM – 9:00 AM

Indication:

Complete pending tasks. Avoid procrastination.

◈ August 11 (Tuesday)

- Tithi: Krishna Ekadashi
- Nakshatra: Punarvasu
- Yoga: Harshana
- Karana: Garaja
- Rahu Kalam: 3:00 PM – 4:30 PM

Indication:

Ekadashi observance strengthens self-control.

◈ August 12 (Wednesday)

- Tithi: Krishna Dwadashi

- Nakshatra: Pushya
- Yoga: Vajra
- Karana: Vanija
- Rahu Kalam: 12:00 PM – 1:30 PM

Indication:

A good day for concluding agreements.

◈ August 13 (Thursday)

- Tithi: Krishna Trayodashi
- Nakshatra: Ashlesha
- Yoga: Siddhi
- Karana: Kaulava
- Rahu Kalam: 1:30 PM – 3:00 PM

Indication:

Pradosha observance. Shiva worship yields merit.

◈ August 14 (Friday)

- Tithi: Krishna Chaturdashi
- Nakshatra: Makam
- Yoga: Variyan
- Karana: Shakuni
- Rahu Kalam: 10:30 AM – 12:00 PM

Indication:

Avoid confrontations. Emotional restraint is advised.

◈ August 15 (Saturday)

- Tithi: Amavasya
- Nakshatra: Pooram
- Yoga: Parigha
- Karana: Chatushpada
- Rahu Kalam: 9:00 AM – 10:30 AM

Indication:

Amavasya. Ideal for charity and inner reflection.

◈ August 16 (Sunday)

- Tithi: Shukla Pratipada
- Nakshatra: Uttaram
- Yoga: Shiva
- Karana: Nagava
- Rahu Kalam: 4:30 PM – 6:00 PM

Indication:

Auspicious day for new beginnings and initiatives.

◈ August 17 (Monday)

- Tithi: Shukla Dwitiya
- Nakshatra: Atham
- Yoga: Siddha
- Karana: Bava
- Rahu Kalam: 7:30 AM – 9:00 AM

Indication:

Progress through cooperation and teamwork.

◈ August 18 (Tuesday)

- Tithi: Shukla Tritiya
- Nakshatra: Chitra
- Yoga: Sadhya
- Karana: Balava
- Rahu Kalam: 3:00 PM – 4:30 PM

Indication:

Creative activities are favored.

◈ August 19 (Wednesday)

- Tithi: Shukla Chaturthi
- Nakshatra: Swati
- Yoga: Shubha
- Karana: Kaulava
- Rahu Kalam: 12:00 PM – 1:30 PM

Indication:

Ganesha worship helps remove obstacles.

◈ August 20 (Thursday)

- Tithi: Shukla Panchami
- Nakshatra: Vishakha
- Yoga: Shobhana
- Karana: Taitila
- Rahu Kalam: 1:30 PM – 3:00 PM

Indication:

Professional matters show improvement.

◈ August 21 (Friday)

- Tithi: Shukla Shashthi
- Nakshatra: Anizham
- Yoga: Atiganda
- Karana: Garaja
- Rahu Kalam: 10:30 AM – 12:00 PM

Indication:

Exercise caution in authority-related matters.

◈ August 22 (Saturday)

- Tithi: Shukla Saptami
- Nakshatra: Jyeshtha
- Yoga: Sukarma
- Karana: Vanija
- Rahu Kalam: 9:00 AM – 10:30 AM

Indication:

Favorable for leadership roles and responsibility.

◈ August 23 (Sunday)

- Tithi: Shukla Ashtami
- Nakshatra: Moola
- Yoga: Dhriti
- Karana: Vishti
- Rahu Kalam: 4:30 PM – 6:00 PM

Indication:

Avoid stress. Maintain emotional balance.

◈ August 24 (Monday)

- Tithi: Shukla Navami
- Nakshatra: Purvashada
- Yoga: Shoola
- Karana: Bava
- Rahu Kalam: 7:30 AM – 9:00 AM

Indication:

Discipline ensures success.

◈ August 25 (Tuesday)

- Tithi: Shukla Dashami
- Nakshatra: Uttarashada
- Yoga: Ganda
- Karana: Balava
- Rahu Kalam: 3:00 PM – 4:30 PM

Indication:

Complete important duties without delay.

◈ August 26 (Wednesday)

- Tithi: Shukla Ekadashi
- Nakshatra: Shravana
- Yoga: Vriddhi
- Karana: Kaulava
- Rahu Kalam: 12:00 PM – 1:30 PM

Indication:

Ekadashi observance enhances clarity and restraint.

◈ August 27 (Thursday)

- Tithi: Shukla Dwadashi
- Nakshatra: Dhanishta
- Yoga: Dhruva
- Karana: Taitila
- Rahu Kalam: 1:30 PM – 3:00 PM

Indication:

A favorable day for settlements and closure.

◈ August 28 (Friday)

- Tithi: Shukla Trayodashi
- Nakshatra: Shatabhisha
- Yoga: Vyaghata
- Karana: Garaja
- Rahu Kalam: 10:30 AM – 12:00 PM

Indication:

Pradosha observance. Shiva worship is beneficial.

◈ August 29 (Saturday)

- Tithi: Shukla Chaturdashi
- Nakshatra: Purvabhadra
- Yoga: Harshana
- Karana: Vanija
- Rahu Kalam: 9:00 AM – 10:30 AM

Indication:

Reflect carefully before commitments.

◈ August 30 (Sunday)

- Tithi: Purnima
- Nakshatra: Uttarabhadra
- Yoga: Vajra
- Karana: Bava
- Rahu Kalam: 4:30 PM – 6:00 PM

Indication:

Purnima. Highly favorable for charity, meditation, and spiritual practices.

⟐ August 31 (Monday)

- Tithi: Krishna Pratipada
- Nakshatra: Revati
- Yoga: Siddhi
- Karana: Balava
- Rahu Kalam: 7:30 AM – 9:00 AM

Indication:

Month concludes. Ideal for review and future planning.

⟐ SEPTEMBER 2026 – DAY TO DAY

(Calculated on the basis of Sunrise)

⟐ September 1 (Tuesday)

- Weekday: Tuesday
- Tithi: Krishna Dwitiya
- Nakshatra: Ashwati
- Yoga: Shubha
- Karana: Kaulava
- Rahu Kalam: 3:00 PM – 4:30 PM

Indication:

Month begins with initiative and energy. Avoid impulsiveness.

◈ September 2 (Wednesday)

- Tithi: Krishna Tritiya
- Nakshatra: Bharani
- Yoga: Shobhana
- Karana: Taitila
- Rahu Kalam: 12:00 PM – 1:30 PM

Indication:

Exercise restraint in speech. Emotional balance is essential.

◈ September 3 (Thursday)

- Tithi: Krishna Chaturthi
- Nakshatra: Krittika
- Yoga: Atiganda
- Karana: Garaja
- Rahu Kalam: 1:30 PM – 3:00 PM

Indication:

Ganesha worship is beneficial. Obstacles reduce gradually.

◈ September 4 (Friday)

- Tithi: Krishna Panchami
- Nakshatra: Rohini
- Yoga: Sukarma
- Karana: Vanija
- Rahu Kalam: 10:30 AM – 12:00 PM

Indication:

Favorable for financial planning and household matters.

◈ September 5 (Saturday)

- Tithi: Krishna Shashthi
- Nakshatra: Mrigashirsha
- Yoga: Dhriti
- Karana: Vishti
- Rahu Kalam: 9:00 AM – 10:30 AM

Indication:

Avoid unnecessary arguments. Maintain patience.

◈ September 6 (Sunday)

- Tithi: Krishna Saptami
- Nakshatra: Ardra
- Yoga: Shoola
- Karana: Bava
- Rahu Kalam: 4:30 PM – 6:00 PM

Indication:

Mental restlessness may occur. Meditation is advised.

◈ September 7 (Monday)

- Tithi: Krishna Ashtami
- Nakshatra: Punarvasu
- Yoga: Ganda
- Karana: Balava
- Rahu Kalam: 7:30 AM – 9:00 AM

Indication:

Efforts yield slow but steady progress.

◈ September 8 (Tuesday)

- Tithi: Krishna Navami
- Nakshatra: Pushya
- Yoga: Vriddhi
- Karana: Kaulava
- Rahu Kalam: 3:00 PM – 4:30 PM

Indication:

Self-confidence improves. Avoid ego conflicts.

◈ September 9 (Wednesday)

- Tithi: Krishna Dashami
- Nakshatra: Ashlesha
- Yoga: Dhruva
- Karana: Taitila
- Rahu Kalam: 12:00 PM – 1:30 PM

Indication:

Good day for completing pending tasks.

◈ September 10 (Thursday)

- Tithi: Krishna Ekadashi
- Nakshatra: Makam
- Yoga: Vyaghata
- Karana: Garaja
- Rahu Kalam: 1:30 PM – 3:00 PM

Indication:

Ekadashi observance strengthens discipline and clarity.

◈ September 11 (Friday)

- Tithi: Krishna Dwadashi
- Nakshatra: Pooram
- Yoga: Harshana
- Karana: Vanija
- Rahu Kalam: 10:30 AM – 12:00 PM

Indication:

Favorable for closure and settlement.

◈ September 12 (Saturday)

- Tithi: Krishna Trayodashi
- Nakshatra: Uttaram
- Yoga: Vajra
- Karana: Kaulava
- Rahu Kalam: 9:00 AM – 10:30 AM

Indication:

Pradosha observance. Shiva worship yields merit.

◈ September 13 (Sunday)

- Tithi: Krishna Chaturdashi
- Nakshatra: Atham
- Yoga: Siddhi
- Karana: Shakuni
- Rahu Kalam: 4:30 PM – 6:00 PM

Indication:

Avoid confrontations. Emotional control is necessary.

◈ September 14 (Monday)

- Tithi: Amavasya
- Nakshatra: Chitra
- Yoga: Variyan
- Karana: Chatushpada
- Rahu Kalam: 7:30 AM – 9:00 AM

Indication:

Amavasya. Suitable for ancestral remembrance and charity.

◈ September 15 (Tuesday)

- Tithi: Shukla Pratipada
- Nakshatra: Swati
- Yoga: Parigha
- Karana: Nagava
- Rahu Kalam: 3:00 PM – 4:30 PM

Indication:

Auspicious for new beginnings and fresh initiatives.

◈ September 16 (Wednesday)

- Tithi: Shukla Dwitiya
- Nakshatra: Vishakha
- Yoga: Shiva
- Karana: Bava
- Rahu Kalam: 12:00 PM – 1:30 PM

Indication:

Partnerships and agreements are favored.

◈ September 17 (Thursday)

- Tithi: Shukla Tritiya
- Nakshatra: Anizham
- Yoga: Siddha
- Karana: Balava
- Rahu Kalam: 1:30 PM – 3:00 PM

Indication:

Efforts bring tangible results. Maintain consistency.

◈ September 18 (Friday)

- Tithi: Shukla Chaturthi
- Nakshatra: Jyeshtha
- Yoga: Sadhya
- Karana: Kaulava
- Rahu Kalam: 10:30 AM – 12:00 PM

Indication:

Ganesha worship removes obstacles.

◈ September 19 (Saturday)

- Tithi: Shukla Panchami
- Nakshatra: Moola
- Yoga: Shubha
- Karana: Taitila
- Rahu Kalam: 9:00 AM – 10:30 AM

Indication:

Favorable for study and strategic planning.

◈ September 20 (Sunday)

- Tithi: Shukla Shashthi
- Nakshatra: Purvashada
- Yoga: Shobhana
- Karana: Garaja
- Rahu Kalam: 4:30 PM – 6:00 PM

Indication:

Self-confidence increases. Avoid dominance.

◈ September 21 (Monday)

- Tithi: Shukla Saptami
- Nakshatra: Uttarashada
- Yoga: Atiganda
- Karana: Vanija
- Rahu Kalam: 7:30 AM – 9:00 AM

Indication:

Work pressure rises. Maintain balance.

◈ September 22 (Tuesday)

- Tithi: Shukla Ashtami
- Nakshatra: Shravana
- Yoga: Sukarma
- Karana: Vishti
- Rahu Kalam: 3:00 PM – 4:30 PM

Indication:

Exercise patience in official matters.

◈ September 23 (Wednesday)

- Tithi: Shukla Navami
- Nakshatra: Dhanishta
- Yoga: Dhriti
- Karana: Bava
- Rahu Kalam: 12:00 PM – 1:30 PM

Indication:

Responsibilities increase. Steady effort is required.

◈ September 24 (Thursday)

- Tithi: Shukla Dashami
- Nakshatra: Shatabhisha
- Yoga: Shoola
- Karana: Balava
- Rahu Kalam: 1:30 PM – 3:00 PM

Indication:

Favorable for concluding long-pending tasks.

◈ September 25 (Friday)

- Tithi: Shukla Ekadashi
- Nakshatra: Purvabhadra
- Yoga: Ganda
- Karana: Kaulava
- Rahu Kalam: 10:30 AM – 12:00 PM

Indication:

Ekadashi observance enhances restraint and clarity.

◈ September 26 (Saturday)

- Tithi: Shukla Dwadashi
- Nakshatra: Uttarabhadra
- Yoga: Vriddhi
- Karana: Taitila
- Rahu Kalam: 9:00 AM – 10:30 AM

Indication:

Good day for settlements and agreements.

◈ September 27 (Sunday)

- Tithi: Shukla Trayodashi
- Nakshatra: Revati
- Yoga: Dhruva
- Karana: Garaja
- Rahu Kalam: 4:30 PM – 6:00 PM

Indication:

Pradosha observance. Shiva worship is beneficial.

◈ September 28 (Monday)

- Tithi: Shukla Chaturdashi
- Nakshatra: Ashwati
- Yoga: Vyaghata
- Karana: Vanija
- Rahu Kalam: 7:30 AM – 9:00 AM

Indication:

Reflect carefully before taking new responsibilities.

◈ September 29 (Tuesday)

- Tithi: Purnima
- Nakshatra: Bharani
- Yoga: Harshana
- Karana: Bava
- Rahu Kalam: 3:00 PM – 4:30 PM

Indication:

Purnima. Favorable for charity and spiritual observances.

◈ September 30 (Wednesday)

- Tithi: Krishna Pratipada
- Nakshatra: Krittika
- Yoga: Vajra
- Karana: Balava
- Rahu Kalam: 12:00 PM – 1:30 PM

Indication:

Month concludes. Ideal for review and future planning.

◈ OCTOBER 2026 – DAY TO DAY

(Calculated on the basis of Sunrise)

◈ October 1 (Thursday)

- Weekday: Thursday

- Tithi: Krishna Dwitiya
- Nakshatra: Rohini
- Yoga: Shubha
- Karana: Kaulava
- Rahu Kalam: 1:30 PM – 3:00 PM

Indication:

Month begins with constructive intent. Favorable for financial planning.

◈ October 2 (Friday)

- Tithi: Krishna Tritiya
- Nakshatra: Mrigashirsha
- Yoga: Shobhana
- Karana: Taitila
- Rahu Kalam: 10:30 AM – 12:00 PM

Indication:

Maintain balance in speech and actions. Avoid misunderstandings.

◈ October 3 (Saturday)

- Tithi: Krishna Chaturthi
- Nakshatra: Ardra
- Yoga: Atiganda
- Karana: Garaja
- Rahu Kalam: 9:00 AM – 10:30 AM

Indication:

Ganesha worship reduces obstacles and delays.

◈ October 4 (Sunday)

- Tithi: Krishna Panchami
- Nakshatra: Punarvasu
- Yoga: Sukarma
- Karana: Vanija
- Rahu Kalam: 4:30 PM – 6:00 PM

Indication:

Favorable for learning and communication.

◈ October 5 (Monday)

- Tithi: Krishna Shashthi
- Nakshatra: Pushya
- Yoga: Dhriti
- Karana: Vishti
- Rahu Kalam: 7:30 AM – 9:00 AM

Indication:

Responsibilities increase. Maintain patience and discipline.

◈ October 6 (Tuesday)

- Tithi: Krishna Saptami
- Nakshatra: Ashlesha
- Yoga: Shoola
- Karana: Bava
- Rahu Kalam: 3:00 PM – 4:30 PM

Indication:

Avoid emotional reactions. Think before responding.

◈ October 7 (Wednesday)

- Tithi: Krishna Ashtami
- Nakshatra: Makam
- Yoga: Ganda
- Karana: Balava
- Rahu Kalam: 12:00 PM – 1:30 PM

Indication:

Mental stress possible. Meditation is beneficial.

◈ October 8 (Thursday)

- Tithi: Krishna Navami
- Nakshatra: Pooram
- Yoga: Vriddhi
- Karana: Kaulava
- Rahu Kalam: 1:30 PM – 3:00 PM

Indication:

Self-confidence increases. Avoid pride.

◈ October 9 (Friday)

- Tithi: Krishna Dashami
- Nakshatra: Uttaram
- Yoga: Dhruva
- Karana: Taitila
- Rahu Kalam: 10:30 AM – 12:00 PM

Indication:

A good day for completing important tasks.

◈ October 10 (Saturday)

- Tithi: Krishna Ekadashi
- Nakshatra: Atham
- Yoga: Vyaghata
- Karana: Garaja
- Rahu Kalam: 9:00 AM – 10:30 AM

Indication:

Ekadashi observance strengthens discipline and clarity.

◈ October 11 (Sunday)

- Tithi: Krishna Dwadashi
- Nakshatra: Chitra
- Yoga: Harshana
- Karana: Vanija
- Rahu Kalam: 4:30 PM – 6:00 PM

Indication:

Favorable for settlement and closure of matters.

◈ October 12 (Monday)

- Tithi: Krishna Trayodashi
- Nakshatra: Swati
- Yoga: Vajra
- Karana: Kaulava
- Rahu Kalam: 7:30 AM – 9:00 AM

Indication:

Pradosha observance. Shiva worship yields merit.

◈ October 13 (Tuesday)

- Tithi: Krishna Chaturdashi
- Nakshatra: Vishakha
- Yoga: Siddhi
- Karana: Shakuni
- Rahu Kalam: 3:00 PM – 4:30 PM

Indication:

Avoid confrontations. Emotional restraint is advised.

◈ October 14 (Wednesday)

- Tithi: Amavasya
- Nakshatra: Anizham
- Yoga: Variyan
- Karana: Chatushpada
- Rahu Kalam: 12:00 PM – 1:30 PM

Indication:

Amavasya. Suitable for ancestral remembrance and charity.

◈ October 15 (Thursday)

- Tithi: Shukla Pratipada
- Nakshatra: Jyeshtha
- Yoga: Parigha
- Karana: Nagava
- Rahu Kalam: 1:30 PM – 3:00 PM

Indication:

Auspicious for new beginnings and planning.

◈ October 16 (Friday)

- Tithi: Shukla Dwitiya
- Nakshatra: Moola
- Yoga: Shiva
- Karana: Bava
- Rahu Kalam: 10:30 AM – 12:00 PM

Indication:

Decisive action yields positive results.

◈ October 17 (Saturday)

- Tithi: Shukla Tritiya
- Nakshatra: Purvashada
- Yoga: Siddha
- Karana: Balava
- Rahu Kalam: 9:00 AM – 10:30 AM

Indication:

Efforts begin to show results. Maintain consistency.

◈ October 18 (Sunday)

- Tithi: Shukla Chaturthi
- Nakshatra: Uttarashada
- Yoga: Sadhya
- Karana: Kaulava
- Rahu Kalam: 4:30 PM – 6:00 PM

Indication:

Ganesha worship removes obstacles.

� October 19 (Monday)

- Tithi: Shukla Panchami
- Nakshatra: Shravana
- Yoga: Shubha
- Karana: Taitila
- Rahu Kalam: 7:30 AM – 9:00 AM

Indication:

Favorable for learning, teaching, and advisory roles.

� October 20 (Tuesday)

- Tithi: Shukla Shashthi
- Nakshatra: Dhanishta
- Yoga: Shobhana
- Karana: Garaja
- Rahu Kalam: 3:00 PM – 4:30 PM

Indication:

Professional recognition is possible.

� October 21 (Wednesday)

- Tithi: Shukla Saptami
- Nakshatra: Shatabhisha
- Yoga: Atiganda
- Karana: Vanija
- Rahu Kalam: 12:00 PM – 1:30 PM

Indication:

Work pressure increases. Maintain balance.

◈ October 22 (Thursday)

- Tithi: Shukla Ashtami
- Nakshatra: Purvabhadra
- Yoga: Sukarma
- Karana: Vishti
- Rahu Kalam: 1:30 PM – 3:00 PM

Indication:

Exercise patience in official matters.

◈ October 23 (Friday)

- Tithi: Shukla Navami
- Nakshatra: Uttarabhadra
- Yoga: Dhriti
- Karana: Bava
- Rahu Kalam: 10:30 AM – 12:00 PM

Indication:

Responsibilities increase. Steady effort brings success.

◈ October 24 (Saturday)

- Tithi: Shukla Dashami
- Nakshatra: Revati
- Yoga: Shoola
- Karana: Balava
- Rahu Kalam: 9:00 AM – 10:30 AM

Indication:

Favorable for completing long-pending duties.

◈ October 25 (Sunday)

- Tithi: Shukla Ekadashi
- Nakshatra: Ashwati
- Yoga: Ganda
- Karana: Kaulava
- Rahu Kalam: 4:30 PM – 6:00 PM

Indication:

Ekadashi observance enhances clarity and restraint.

◈ October 26 (Monday)

- Tithi: Shukla Dwadashi
- Nakshatra: Bharani
- Yoga: Vriddhi
- Karana: Taitila
- Rahu Kalam: 7:30 AM – 9:00 AM

Indication:

A good day for agreements and settlements.

◈ October 27 (Tuesday)

- Tithi: Shukla Trayodashi
- Nakshatra: Krittika
- Yoga: Dhruva
- Karana: Garaja
- Rahu Kalam: 3:00 PM – 4:30 PM

Indication:

Pradosha observance. Shiva worship is beneficial.

◈ October 28 (Wednesday)

- Tithi: Shukla Chaturdashi
- Nakshatra: Rohini
- Yoga: Vyaghata
- Karana: Vanija
- Rahu Kalam: 12:00 PM – 1:30 PM

Indication:

Reflect carefully before making commitments.

◈ October 29 (Thursday)

- Tithi: Purnima
- Nakshatra: Mrigashirsha
- Yoga: Harshana
- Karana: Bava
- Rahu Kalam: 1:30 PM – 3:00 PM

Indication:

Purnima. Highly favorable for charity and spiritual practices.

◈ October 30 (Friday)

- Tithi: Krishna Pratipada
- Nakshatra: Ardra
- Yoga: Vajra
- Karana: Balava
- Rahu Kalam: 10:30 AM – 12:00 PM

Indication:

Review decisions and plan ahead calmly.

◈ October 31 (Saturday)

- Tithi: Krishna Dwitiya
- Nakshatra: Punarvasu
- Yoga: Siddhi
- Karana: Kaulava
- Rahu Kalaṃ: 9:00 AM – 10:30 AM

Indication:

Month concludes. Discipline and foresight ensure stability.

◈ NOVEMBER 2026 – DAY TO DAY

(Calculated on the basis of Sunrise)

◈ November 1 (Sunday)

Weekday: Sunday

Tithi: Krishna Tritiya

Nakshatra: Pushya

Yoga: Shubha

Karana: Taitila

Rahu Kalam: 4:30 PM – 6:00 PM

Indication:

Month begins with clarity of purpose. Favorable for household decisions.

◈ November 2 (Monday)

Tithi: Krishna Chaturthi

Nakshatra: Ashlesha

Yoga: Shobhana

Karana: Garaja

Rahu Kalam: 7:30 AM – 9:00 AM

Indication:

Ganesha worship removes obstacles. Avoid emotional reactions.

◈ November 3 (Tuesday)

Tithi: Krishna Panchami

Nakshatra: Makam

Yoga: Atiganda

Karana: Vanija

Rahu Kalam: 3:00 PM – 4:30 PM

Indication:

Exercise caution in authority-related matters. Maintain humility.

◈ November 4 (Wednesday)

Tithi: Krishna Shashthi

Nakshatra: Pooram

Yoga: Sukarma

Karana: Vishti

Rahu Kalam: 12:00 PM – 1:30 PM

Indication:

Favorable for creative work and planning.

◈ November 5 (Thursday)

Tithi: Krishna Saptami

Nakshatra: Uttaram

Yoga: Dhriti

Karana: Bava

Rahu Kalam: 1:30 PM – 3:00 PM

Indication:

Guidance from elders proves beneficial.

◈ November 6 (Friday)

Tithi: Krishna Ashtami

Nakshatra: Atham

Yoga: Shoola

Karana: Balava

Rahu Kalam: 10:30 AM – 12:00 PM

Indication:

Avoid unnecessary confrontations. Maintain restraint.

◈ November 7 (Saturday)

Tithi: Krishna Navami

Nakshatra: Chitra

Yoga: Ganda

Karana: Kaulava

Rahu Kalam: 9:00 AM – 10:30 AM

Indication:

Patience is required. Results may be delayed.

◈ November 8 (Sunday)

Tithi: Krishna Dashami

Nakshatra: Swati

Yoga: Vriddhi

Karana: Taitila

Rahu Kalam: 4:30 PM – 6:00 PM

Indication:

Self-confidence improves. Avoid overconfidence.

◈ November 9 (Monday)

Tithi: Krishna Ekadashi

Nakshatra: Vishakha

Yoga: Dhruva

Karana: Garaja

Rahu Kalam: 7:30 AM – 9:00 AM

Indication:

Ekadashi observance enhances discipline and clarity.

◈ November 10 (Tuesday)

Tithi: Krishna Dwadashi

Nakshatra: Anizham

Yoga: Vyaghata

Karana: Vanija

Rahu Kalam: 3:00 PM – 4:30 PM

Indication:

Favorable for completing pending tasks.

◈ November 11 (Wednesday)

Tithi: Krishna Trayodashi

Nakshatra: Jyeshtha

Yoga: Harshana

Karana: Kaulava

Rahu Kalam: 12:00 PM – 1:30 PM

Indication:

Pradosha observance. Shiva worship yields merit.

◈ November 12 (Thursday)

Tithi: Krishna Chaturdashi

Nakshatra: Moola

Yoga: Vajra

Karana: Shakuni

Rahu Kalam: 1:30 PM – 3:00 PM

Indication:

Avoid confrontations. Emotional control is necessary.

◈ November 13 (Friday)

Tithi: Amavasya

Nakshatra: Purvashada

Yoga: Siddhi

Karana: Chatushpada

Rahu Kalam: 10:30 AM – 12:00 PM

Indication:

Amavasya. Suitable for ancestral remembrance and charity.

◈ November 14 (Saturday)

Tithi: Shukla Pratipada

Nakshatra: Uttarashada

Yoga: Variyan

Karana: Nagava

Rahu Kalam: 9:00 AM – 10:30 AM

Indication:

Auspicious for new beginnings and planning.

◈ November 15 (Sunday)

Tithi: Shukla Dwitiya

Nakshatra: Shravana

Yoga: Parigha

Karana: Bava

Rahu Kalam: 4:30 PM – 6:00 PM

Indication:

Learning and advisory activities are favored.

◈ November 16 (Monday)

Tithi: Shukla Tritiya

Nakshatra: Dhanishta

Yoga: Shiva

Karana: Balava

Rahu Kalam: 7:30 AM – 9:00 AM

Indication:

Decisive action yields positive outcomes.

◈ November 17 (Tuesday)

Tithi: Shukla Chaturthi

Nakshatra: Shatabhisha

Yoga: Siddha

Karana: Kaulava

Rahu Kalam: 3:00 PM – 4:30 PM

Indication:

Ganesha worship removes obstacles.

◈ November 18 (Wednesday)

Tithi: Shukla Panchami

Nakshatra: Purvabhadra

Yoga: Sadhya

Karana: Taitila

Rahu Kalam: 12:00 PM – 1:30 PM

Indication:

Progress through consistency and patience.

◈ November 19 (Thursday)

Tithi: Shukla Shashthi

Nakshatra: Uttarabhadra

Yoga: Shubha

Karana: Garaja

Rahu Kalam: 1:30 PM – 3:00 PM

Indication:

Favorable for assuming responsibility.

◈ November 20 (Friday)

Tithi: Shukla Saptami

Nakshatra: Revati

Yoga: Shobhana

Karana: Vanija

Rahu Kalam: 10:30 AM – 12:00 PM

Indication:

Professional recognition is possible.

◈ November 21 (Saturday)

Tithi: Shukla Ashtami

Nakshatra: Ashwati

Yoga: Atiganda

Karana: Vishti

Rahu Kalam: 9:00 AM – 10:30 AM

Indication:

Exercise patience in stressful situations.

◈ November 22 (Sunday)

Tithi: Shukla Navami

Nakshatra: Bharani

Yoga: Sukarma

Karana: Bava

Rahu Kalam: 4:30 PM – 6:00 PM

Indication:

Self-confidence improves. Avoid dominance.

◈ November 23 (Monday)

Tithi: Shukla Dashami

Nakshatra: Krittika

Yoga: Dhriti

Karana: Balava

Rahu Kalam: 7:30 AM – 9:00 AM

Indication:

Complete important responsibilities diligently.

◈ November 24 (Tuesday)

Tithi: Shukla Ekadashi

Nakshatra: Rohini

Yoga: Shoola

Karana: Kaulava

Rahu Kalam: 3:00 PM – 4:30 PM

Indication:

Ekadashi observance enhances restraint and clarity.

◈ November 25 (Wednesday)

Tithi: Shukla Dwadashi

Nakshatra: Mrigashirsha

Yoga: Ganda

Karana: Taitila

Rahu Kalam: 12:00 PM – 1:30 PM

Indication:

A good day for settlements and agreements.

◈ November 26 (Thursday)

Tithi: Shukla Trayodashi

Nakshatra: Ardra

Yoga: Vriddhi

Karana: Garaja

Rahu Kalam: 1:30 PM – 3:00 PM

Indication:

Pradosha observance. Shiva worship is beneficial.

◈ November 27 (Friday)

Tithi: Shukla Chaturdashi

Nakshatra: Punarvasu

Yoga: Dhruva

Karana: Vanija

Rahu Kalam: 10:30 AM – 12:00 PM

Indication:

Reflect carefully before major commitments.

◈ November 28 (Saturday)

Tithi: Purnima

Nakshatra: Pushya

Yoga: Vyaghata

Karana: Bava

Rahu Kalam: 9:00 AM – 10:30 AM

Indication:

Purnima. Highly favorable for charity and spiritual practices.

◈ November 29 (Sunday)

Tithi: Krishna Pratipada

Nakshatra: Ashlesha

Yoga: Harshana

Karana: Balava

Rahu Kalam: 4:30 PM – 6:00 PM

Indication:

Begin review of recent actions. Plan corrections.

◈ November 30 (Monday)

Tithi: Krishna Dwitiya

Nakshatra: Makam

Yoga: Vajra

Karana: Kaulava

Rahu Kalam: 7:30 AM – 9:00 AM

Indication:

Month concludes. Discipline and foresight ensure stability.

◈ DECEMBER 2026 – DAY TO DAY

(Calculated on the basis of Sunrise)

◈ December 1 (Tuesday)

- Weekday: Tuesday
- Tithi: Krishna Tritiya
- Nakshatra: Pooram
- Yoga: Shubha
- Karana: Taitila
- Rahu Kalam: 3:00 PM – 4:30 PM

Indication:

Month begins with renewed energy. Direct efforts toward meaningful goals.

◈ December 2 (Wednesday)

- Tithi: Krishna Chaturthi
- Nakshatra: Uttaram
- Yoga: Shobhana
- Karana: Garaja
- Rahu Kalam: 12:00 PM – 1:30 PM

Indication:

Ganesha worship removes obstacles. Favorable for planning.

◈ December 3 (Thursday)

- Tithi: Krishna Panchami
- Nakshatra: Atham
- Yoga: Atiganda
- Karana: Vanija
- Rahu Kalam: 1:30 PM – 3:00 PM

Indication:

Exercise restraint in speech. Avoid unnecessary arguments.

◈ December 4 (Friday)

- Tithi: Krishna Shashthi
- Nakshatra: Chitra
- Yoga: Sukarma
- Karana: Vishti
- Rahu Kalam: 10:30 AM – 12:00 PM

Indication:

Favorable for creative and artistic activities.

◈ December 5 (Saturday)

- Tithi: Krishna Saptami
- Nakshatra: Swati
- Yoga: Dhriti
- Karana: Bava
- Rahu Kalam: 9:00 AM – 10:30 AM

Indication:

Patience and diplomacy bring success.

◈ December 6 (Sunday)

- Tithi: Krishna Ashtami
- Nakshatra: Vishakha
- Yoga: Shoola
- Karana: Balava
- Rahu Kalam: 4:30 PM – 6:00 PM

Indication:

Avoid impulsive decisions. Reflect before acting.

◈ December 7 (Monday)

- Tithi: Krishna Navami
- Nakshatra: Anizham
- Yoga: Ganda
- Karana: Kaulava
- Rahu Kalam: 7:30 AM – 9:00 AM

Indication:

Hard work is necessary. Results may be delayed but assured.

◈ December 8 (Tuesday)

- Tithi: Krishna Dashami
- Nakshatra: Jyeshtha
- Yoga: Vriddhi
- Karana: Taitila
- Rahu Kalam: 3:00 PM – 4:30 PM

Indication:

Self-confidence increases. Avoid dominance.

◈ December 9 (Wednesday)

- Tithi: Krishna Ekadashi
- Nakshatra: Moola
- Yoga: Dhruva
- Karana: Garaja
- Rahu Kalam: 12:00 PM – 1:30 PM

Indication:

Ekadashi observance enhances clarity and restraint.

◈ December 10 (Thursday)

- Tithi: Krishna Dwadashi
- Nakshatra: Purvashada
- Yoga: Vyaghata
- Karana: Vanija
- Rahu Kalam: 1:30 PM – 3:00 PM

Indication:

Favorable for completing pending responsibilities.

◈ December 11 (Friday)

- Tithi: Krishna Trayodashi
- Nakshatra: Uttarashada
- Yoga: Harshana
- Karana: Kaulava
- Rahu Kalam: 10:30 AM – 12:00 PM

Indication:

Pradosha observance. Shiva worship yields merit.

◈ December 12 (Saturday)

- Tithi: Krishna Chaturdashi
- Nakshatra: Shravana
- Yoga: Vajra
- Karana: Shakuni
- Rahu Kalam: 9:00 AM – 10:30 AM

Indication:

Avoid confrontations. Emotional balance is essential.

◈ December 13 (Sunday)

- Tithi: Amavasya
- Nakshatra: Dhanishta
- Yoga: Siddhi
- Karana: Chatushpada
- Rahu Kalam: 4:30 PM – 6:00 PM

Indication:

Amavasya. Ideal for charity, introspection, and ancestral remembrance.

◈ December 14 (Monday)

- Tithi: Shukla Pratipada
- Nakshatra: Shatabhisha
- Yoga: Variyan
- Karana: Nagava
- Rahu Kalam: 7:30 AM – 9:00 AM

Indication:

Auspicious for new beginnings and restructuring plans.

◈ December 15 (Tuesday)

- Tithi: Shukla Dwitiya
- Nakshatra: Purvabhadra
- Yoga: Parigha
- Karana: Bava
- Rahu Kalam: 3:00 PM – 4:30 PM

Indication:

Cooperation and teamwork bring success.

◈ December 16 (Wednesday)

- Tithi: Shukla Tritiya
- Nakshatra: Uttarabhadra
- Yoga: Shiva
- Karana: Balava
- Rahu Kalam: 12:00 PM – 1:30 PM

Indication:

Decisive actions lead to progress.

◈ December 17 (Thursday)

- Tithi: Shukla Chaturthi
- Nakshatra: Revati
- Yoga: Siddha
- Karana: Kaulava
- Rahu Kalam: 1:30 PM – 3:00 PM

Indication:

Ganesha worship removes obstacles and delays.

◈ December 18 (Friday)

- Tithi: Shukla Panchami
- Nakshatra: Ashwati
- Yoga: Sadhya
- Karana: Taitila
- Rahu Kalam: 10:30 AM – 12:00 PM

Indication:

Initiatives taken now yield positive results.

◈ December 19 (Saturday)

- Tithi: Shukla Shashthi
- Nakshatra: Bharani
- Yoga: Shubha
- Karana: Garaja
- Rahu Kalam: 9:00 AM – 10:30 AM

Indication:

Responsibility increases. Act with discipline.

◈ December 20 (Sunday)

- Tithi: Shukla Saptami
- Nakshatra: Krittika
- Yoga: Shobhana
- Karana: Vanija
- Rahu Kalam: 4:30 PM – 6:00 PM

Indication:

Self-confidence improves. Avoid overexertion.

◈ December 21 (Monday)

- Tithi: Shukla Ashtami
- Nakshatra: Rohini
- Yoga: Atiganda
- Karana: Vishti
- Rahu Kalam: 7:30 AM – 9:00 AM

Indication:

Maintain emotional balance. Avoid stress.

◈ December 22 (Tuesday)

- Tithi: Shukla Navami
- Nakshatra: Mrigashirsha
- Yoga: Sukarma
- Karana: Bava
- Rahu Kalam: 3:00 PM – 4:30 PM

Indication:

Favorable for learning, writing, and communication.

◈ December 23 (Wednesday)

- Tithi: Shukla Dashami
- Nakshatra: Ardra
- Yoga: Dhriti
- Karana: Balava
- Rahu Kalam: 12:00 PM – 1:30 PM

Indication:

Complete important duties carefully.

◈ December 24 (Thursday)

- Tithi: Shukla Ekadashi
- Nakshatra: Punarvasu
- Yoga: Shoola
- Karana: Kaulava
- Rahu Kalam: 1:30 PM – 3:00 PM

Indication:

Ekadashi observance enhances restraint and mental clarity.

◈ December 25 (Friday)

- Tithi: Shukla Dwadashi
- Nakshatra: Pushya
- Yoga: Ganda
- Karana: Taitila
- Rahu Kalam: 10:30 AM – 12:00 PM

Indication:

A good day for settlements and agreements.

◈ December 26 (Saturday)

- Tithi: Shukla Trayodashi
- Nakshatra: Ashlesha
- Yoga: Vriddhi
- Karana: Garaja
- Rahu Kalam: 9:00 AM – 10:30 AM

Indication:

Pradosha observance. Shiva worship yields merit.

◈ December 27 (Sunday)

- Tithi: Shukla Chaturdashi
- Nakshatra: Makam
- Yoga: Dhruva
- Karana: Vanija
- Rahu Kalam: 4:30 PM – 6:00 PM

Indication:

Reflect carefully before making long-term commitments.

◈ December 28 (Monday)

- Tithi: Purnima
- Nakshatra: Pooram
- Yoga: Vyaghata
- Karana: Bava
- Rahu Kalam: 7:30 AM – 9:00 AM

Indication:

Purnima. Highly favorable for charity, meditation, and spiritual observances.

◈ December 29 (Tuesday)

- Tithi: Krishna Pratipada
- Nakshatra: Uttaram
- Yoga: Harshana
- Karana: Balava
- Rahu Kalam: 3:00 PM – 4:30 PM

Indication:

Begin year-end review. Prepare for transition.

◈ December 30 (Wednesday)

- Tithi: Krishna Dwitiya
- Nakshatra: Atham
- Yoga: Vajra
- Karana: Kaulava
- Rahu Kalam: 12:00 PM – 1:30 PM

Indication:

Discipline and foresight ensure stability.

◈ December 31 (Thursday)

- Tithi: Krishna Tritiya
- Nakshatra: Chitra
- Yoga: Siddhi
- Karana: Taitila
- Rahu Kalam: 1:30 PM – 3:00 PM

Indication:

Year concludes. Reflect deeply and prepare for renewal.

CHAPTER 4 - ECLIPSES, SACRED VOWS, AND SPECIAL OBSERVANCES – 2026

4.1 The Astrological and Ritual Meaning of Eclipses

Eclipses (*Grahanas*) are among the most significant phenomena in Panchanga science.

They are not treated merely as astronomical events, but as **periods of intensified karmic activity**, during which subtle disturbances occur in the natural order.

According to traditional understanding:

- **Solar Eclipse (Surya Grahana):**
  Affects authority, vitality, governance, and social order.
- **Lunar Eclipse (Chandra Grahana):**
  Affects the mind, emotions, public sentiment, and domestic harmony.

During eclipses:

- Auspicious activities are avoided
- Worship, japa, and meditation are recommended
- Charity performed after an eclipse yields multiplied merit

4.2 Sutaka Kala (Period of Ritual Restraint)

Sutaka refers to the preparatory period before an eclipse.

Sutaka Rules:

- **Solar Eclipse:** Sutaka begins **12 hours before** the eclipse
- **Lunar Eclipse:** Sutaka begins **9 hours before** the eclipse

During Sutaka:

- Cooking and eating are avoided
- Temple rituals are suspended
- Normal household activity is minimized

Sutaka applies to all except:

- Children
- The elderly
- The sick

4.3 Eclipses Occurring in 2026

◈ Solar Eclipses – 2026

1. Solar Eclipse – March 29, 2026

- **Type:** Partial Solar Eclipse
- **Visibility:** Not visible in India
- **Ritual Impact in India:**
  Sutaka rules **do not apply**, as the eclipse is not visible.

Significance:

Though invisible, it indicates subtle shifts in leadership and administrative matters globally.

---

2. Solar Eclipse – September 21, 2026

- **Type:** Partial Solar Eclipse

- **Visibility:** Not visible in India
- **Ritual Impact:**
  No Sutaka observance required in India.

Significance:

Associated with restructuring tendencies in governance and institutional systems.

○ **Lunar Eclipses – 2026**

1. Lunar Eclipse – March 14, 2026

- **Type:** Partial Lunar Eclipse
- **Visibility:** Visible in India

Ritual Instructions:

- Sutaka applies (9 hours prior)
- Fasting is recommended
- Avoid sleeping during the eclipse
- Perform mantra japa and meditation

Charity after the eclipse is highly auspicious.

---

2. Lunar Eclipse – September 7, 2026

- **Type:** Partial Lunar Eclipse
- **Visibility:** Visible in India

Ritual Instructions:

Same as above. Special emphasis on mental discipline and charity.

4.4 Conduct During an Eclipse

Recommended Practices:

- Chanting of divine names
- Reading of sacred texts
- Silent meditation

Prohibited Activities:

- Eating and cooking
- Travel for auspicious purposes
- Initiating new ventures

After the eclipse:

- Bathing is mandatory
- Homes and temples are ritually purified
- Charity (food, clothing, money) is recommended

4.5 Sacred Monthly Vows (Vratas) in 2026

Ekadashi Vrata

Observed on the 11th lunar day of each fortnight.

Benefits:

- Mental clarity
- Self-discipline
- Reduction of negative karmic tendencies

Fasting may be:

- Complete
- Fruit-based

- Water-based

According to individual capacity.

Pradosha Vrata

Observed on the 13th lunar day (Trayodashi), especially when it falls on a **Monday or Saturday**.

Significance:

- Worship of Lord Shiva
- Removal of obstacles
- Stability in life and career

Amavasya Observances

New Moon days are reserved for:

- Ancestral remembrance (*Pitru Karma*)
- Charity
- Self-reflection

Amavasya is **not** suitable for initiating new ventures.

Purnima Observances

Full Moon days are ideal for:

- Charity
- Spiritual vows
- Completion of religious observances

4.6 Maha Shivaratri – 2026

Date: February 15, 2026

Maha Shivaratri is one of the most powerful nights for spiritual practice.

Observances:

- Night-long vigil (*Jagaranam*)
- Abhishekam to Lord Shiva
- Fasting and mantra chanting

Spiritual Effect:

Enhances inner purity, discipline, and clarity of purpose.

4.7 General Guidance for Sacred Observances

- Rituals must be aligned with **Tithi and Nakshatra**, not civil dates
- Purity of intention is more important than ritual complexity
- Charity performed with humility multiplies merit

CONCLUSION OF PART 4

Eclipses and sacred observances serve as **periodic reminders of cosmic order**.

When respected with awareness and discipline, they purify both individual life and collective consciousness.

CHAPTER 5 - MUHURTAS (AUSPICIOUS TIMINGS) – 2026

5.1 Concept of Muhurta in Panchanga

A *Muhurta* is a carefully chosen time window during which cosmic forces are harmonized to support a specific human activity.

In Panchanga science, success is not attributed to effort alone, but to **effort undertaken at the right time**.

A Muhurta is judged primarily by:

- Tithi
- Nakshatra
- Yoga
- Karana
- Weekday
- Strength of benefic planets

Even a small activity, when performed at a favorable Muhurta, yields lasting results.

5.2 Abhijit Muhurta

Abhijit Muhurta is universally auspicious and free from most defects.

- Occurs around **midday**, excluding Wednesdays
- Suitable for almost all activities except marriage

Applications:

- Starting important work

- Signing agreements
- Crisis intervention
- Administrative decisions

Abhijit Muhurta is especially useful when no other auspicious time is available.

5.3 Marriage Muhurta (Vivaha Muhurta) – 2026

Favorable Conditions:

- Shukla Paksha preferred
- Benefic Nakshatras such as:
    - Rohini
    - Mrigashirsha
    - Uttara Phalguni
    - Hasta
    - Swati
    - Anuradha
    - Revati

Avoid:

- Chaturthi, Shashthi, Ashtami, Navami
- Amavasya and Purnima
- Rahu Kalam, Yamagandam, Gulika

Note:

Final marriage Muhurta must always be fixed after examining the horoscopes of both individuals.

5.4 Griha Pravesha Muhurta (House Entry)

Highly Favorable:

- Shukla Paksha
- Fixed and gentle Nakshatras:
    - Rohini
    - Uttara Phalguni
    - Uttarashada
    - Uttarabhadra

Avoid:

- Tuesday and Saturday
- Amavasya
- Eclipse days

Purpose:

Ensures peace, prosperity, and stability in the household.

5.5 Naming Ceremony (Namakarana Muhurta)

Recommended:

- 10th, 11th, or 12th day after birth
- Auspicious Nakshatras:
    - Rohini
    - Pushya
    - Hasta
    - Revati

Avoid:

- Birth Nakshatra if malefic
- Rahu Kalam

Benefit:

Supports health, longevity, and positive character traits.

5.6 Annaprashana Muhurta (First Feeding)

Ideal Age:

- 6th or 8th month

Auspicious Nakshatras:

- Rohini
- Mrigashirsha
- Pushya
- Anuradha

Avoid:

- Eclipse days
- Amavasya

5.7 Vidyarambha Muhurta (Initiation into Learning)

Best Period:

- During **Navaratri**
- On **Vijaya Dashami**

Auspicious Nakshatras:

- Hasta
- Pushya
- Swati

Purpose:

Ensures clarity of intellect and sustained interest in learning.

5.8 Business and Career Muhurtas

Suitable for:

- Starting business ventures
- Opening shops
- Signing contracts
- Joining new employment

Favorable Nakshatras:

- Uttara Phalguni
- Hasta
- Chitra
- Anuradha

Avoid:

- Rahu Kalam
- Amavasya
- Eclipse days

5.9 Travel Muhurta

Favorable Days:

- Monday
- Wednesday
- Thursday

Favorable Nakshatras:

- Ashwini
- Pushya
- Swati

Avoid:

- Travel during Rahu Kalam
- Travel on Amavasya for major journeys

5.10 Medical and Surgical Muhurtas

Preferred:

- Krishna Paksha
- Avoid Moon transiting the afflicted body part's sign

Avoid:

- Amavasya
- Purnima
- Eclipse days

5.11 General Prohibited Periods (Sarva Varjya)

Activities should be avoided during:

- Rahu Kalam
- Yamagandam
- Gulika Kalam

- Eclipse periods
- Sutaka Kala

CHAPTER 6 - ANNUAL ZODIAC PREDICTIONS – 2026

(Sidereal / Nirayana System)

♈ Aries (Mesha)

General:

2026 emphasizes responsibility and disciplined growth. Impulsive tendencies must be restrained.

Career & Finance:

Steady progress through sustained effort. Avoid speculative ventures. Gains improve after mid-year.

Relationships:

Patience is essential. Avoid dominance in personal matters.

Health:

Minor fatigue possible. Regular routine is advised.

♉ Taurus (Vrishabha)

General:

A year of consolidation and material stability. Long-term planning yields success.

Career & Finance:

Financial security improves. Favorable for property and savings.

Relationships:

Harmony prevails. Family support strengthens.

Health:

Generally sound. Maintain dietary discipline.

♊ Gemini (Mithuna)

General:

A dynamic year requiring mental focus. Avoid scattering energies.

Career & Finance:

Opportunities arise through communication and networking. Income fluctuates initially.

Relationships:

Clear communication prevents misunderstandings.

Health:

Stress-related issues possible. Adequate rest is necessary.

♋ Cancer (Karka)

General:

Emotional maturity is tested. Inner strength becomes a key asset.

Career & Finance:

Professional responsibilities increase. Financial growth is gradual.

Relationships:

Family matters demand attention. Emotional balance is vital.

Health:

Digestive sensitivity possible. Mindful eating helps.

♌ Leo (Simha)

General:

Leadership opportunities emerge. Ego must be balanced with humility.

Career & Finance:

Recognition is possible. Avoid risky financial commitments.

Relationships:

Mutual respect strengthens bonds.

Health:

Vitality remains good. Avoid overexertion.

♍ Virgo (Kanya)

General:

A year of methodical progress and refinement.

Career & Finance:

Favorable for analytical and service-oriented roles. Financial discipline brings stability.

Relationships:

Practical support strengthens relationships.

Health:

Nervous tension possible. Maintain mental calm.

♎ Libra (Tula)

General:

Balance and fairness define the year. Decision-making improves with clarity.

Career & Finance:

Partnerships bring growth. Legal and contractual matters favor resolution.

Relationships:

Harmony improves. Avoid indecision.

Health:

Generally stable. Maintain physical activity.

♏ Scorpio (Vrischika)

General:

Transformation through discipline. Avoid secrecy and rigidity.

Career & Finance:

Professional challenges lead to growth. Financial caution advised.

Relationships:

Emotional depth increases. Avoid possessiveness.

Health:

Stress management is essential.

♐ Sagittarius (Dhanu)

General:

Expansion through learning and self-development.

Career & Finance:

Educational, advisory, and travel-related fields prosper. Financial growth improves later in the year.

Relationships:

Optimism strengthens bonds.

Health:

Good vitality. Maintain moderation.

♑ Capricorn (Makara)

General:

A year demanding perseverance and responsibility.

Career & Finance:

Professional consolidation. Long-term investments favored.

Relationships:

Practical approach benefits family life.

Health:

Joint and bone care required.

♒ Aquarius (Kumbha)

General:

Innovation balanced with realism brings success.

Career & Finance:

Opportunities in technology and social initiatives. Avoid impulsive expenses.

Relationships:

Friendships play a key role.

Health:

Maintain circulation and nervous system health.

♓ Pisces (Meena)

General:

Spiritual inclination increases. Intuition guides decisions.

Career & Finance:

Creative and healing professions benefit. Financial discipline required.

Relationships:

Compassion deepens relationships.

Health:

Emotional well-being is crucial. Meditation is beneficial.

CHAPTER 7 - NAKSHATRA-BASED ANNUAL ANALYSIS – 2026

(Sidereal / Nirayana System)

7.1 Role of Nakshatra in Annual Prediction

While zodiac signs describe broad tendencies, **Nakshatras reveal precise karmic experience.**

Annual Nakshatra analysis focuses on:

- Mental state and emotional resilience
- Results of effort
- Timing of gains and obstacles
- Inner spiritual evolution

In 2026, Saturn's karmic discipline and Jupiter's guiding influence make Nakshatra-based reading especially significant.

7.2 Nakshatra-wise Predictions

◈ Ashwini

Theme: Initiation and momentum

A year favorable for beginnings. Avoid haste. Health improves with discipline.

◈ Bharani

Theme: Responsibility and restraint

Challenges refine character. Patience brings eventual success.

◈ **Krittika**

Theme: Purification and clarity

Cutting away excess is necessary. Career clarity improves after mid-year.

◈ **Rohini**

Theme: Growth and prosperity

Material gains possible. Guard against attachment and complacency.

◈ **Mrigashirsha**

Theme: Search and adaptation

Frequent changes. Success through flexibility and learning.

◈ **Ardra**

Theme: Transformation through intensity

Emotional upheavals possible. Inner strength emerges through discipline.

◈ **Punarvasu**

Theme: Renewal and recovery

Lost opportunities return. A favorable year for stability.

◈ **Pushya**

Theme: Nourishment and authority

Professional respect increases. Leadership responsibilities expand.

◈ **Ashlesha**

Theme: Control and awareness

Avoid manipulation—internal or external. Spiritual growth through self-honesty.

◈ Magha

Theme: Ancestral duty and authority

Family and lineage matters dominate. Respect for tradition brings strength.

◈ Purva Phalguni

Theme: Enjoyment and creativity

Pleasures increase. Balance indulgence with responsibility.

◈ Uttara Phalguni

Theme: Commitment and contracts

Favorable for long-term alliances and marriage-related matters.

◈ Hasta

Theme: Skill and execution

Hands-on effort brings results. A productive and practical year.

◈ Chitra

Theme: Design and ambition

Recognition through creativity. Avoid ego conflicts.

◈ Swati

Theme: Independence and movement

Travel and change indicated. Maintain grounding and discipline.

◈ Vishakha

Theme: Determination and achievement

Strong drive for success. Avoid obsession with outcomes.

◈ Anuradha

Theme: Cooperation and loyalty

Support from friends and networks. Steady progress assured.

◈ Jyeshtha

Theme: Authority and responsibility

Leadership tested. Humility ensures stability.

◈ Moola

Theme: Root-level change

Major restructuring possible. Let go of outdated patterns.

◈ Purva Ashada

Theme: Victory through persistence

Delayed success materializes. Moral discipline is essential.

◈ Uttara Ashada

Theme: Endurance and righteousness

Long-term gains. Reputation strengthens through ethical conduct.

◈ Shravana

Theme: Learning and transmission

Education, teaching, and advisory roles prosper.

◈ Dhanishta

Theme: Rhythm and ambition

Financial movement increases. Balance ambition with harmony.

◈ Shatabhisha

Theme: Healing and detachment

Solitude aids clarity. Health awareness improves.

◈ Purva Bhadrapada

Theme: Intensity and idealism

Strong beliefs tested. Channel passion constructively.

◈ Uttara Bhadrapada

Theme: Stability and depth

Spiritual grounding increases. Quiet progress brings lasting peace.

◈ Revati

Theme: Completion and compassion

Endings lead to fulfillment. Favorable for spiritual closure and guidance.

7.3 General Nakshatra Guidance for 2026

- **Saturn-affected Nakshatras** must emphasize patience and duty
- **Jupiter-ruled Nakshatras** benefit from education and ethical conduct
- Eclipse-influenced Nakshatras should increase charity and introspection

CHAPTER 8 - SHAKTI PUJAS – STAR-WISE, MONTH-WISE FOR THE YEAR 2026

◈ TABLE OF STARS-SHAKTI FORM-CORE INTENTION:

BITH STAR	SHAKTI FORM	CORE INTENTION
Ashwini Bharani Krittika	Durga	Protection, health
Rohini Mrigashirsha Ardra	Katyayani	Courage, decisiveness
Punarvasu Pushya Ashlesha	Chandika	Removal of fear
Magha Phalguni Uttara	Mahakali	Authority, ancestral strength
Hasta Chitra Swati	Durga	Stability
Vishakha Anuradha Jyeshtha	Katyayani	Victory over opposition
Moola Ashada Uttara Ashada	Chandika	Destruction of obstacles
Shravana Dhanishta Shatabhisha	Mahakali	Discipline
Purva Uttara Bhadra Revati	Durga	Inner protection

◈ JANUARY 2026 – SHAKTI OF PROTECTION

Presiding Energy: *Durga / Katyayani*

Mantra:

� ��� �������� ���

� FEBRUARY 2026 – SHAKTI OF DISCIPLINE

Presiding Energy: *Mahakali*

Birth Star Group Shakti

All Stars Mahakali

Special note: Ideal month for Sade-Sati, Kantaka Shani, Ashtama Shani natives.

Mantra:

� ����� �������� ���

� MARCH 2026 – SHAKTI OF KNOWLEDGE

Presiding Energy: Saraswati

Birth Star

Ashwini – Rohini – Pushya – Hasta – Shravana – Revati

Shakti Form: Saraswati

Others Matangi

Mantra:

� �� ��������� ��� Mantra:

� �� ��������� ���

� APRIL 2026 – SHAKTI OF INITIATION

Presiding Energy: *Lalita / Tripurasundari*

Birth Star	Shakti
Fire & Air Nakshatras	Tripurasundari
Water & Earth Nakshatras	Lalita Devi

Mantra:

� ����� ����� �����
���������������� ���

� MAY 2026 – SHAKTI OF VICTORY

Presiding Energy: Bagalamukhi

Birth Star Group

Jyeshtha – Vishakha – Moola – Shatabhisha

Focus:Enemy suppression

Others Durga

Mantra:

� ����� ���������� ���

� JUNE 2026 – SHAKTI OF HEALING

Presiding Energy: Dhumavati / Tara

Birth Star:

Ardra – Ashlesha – Moola – Purva Bhadra

Shakti:Dhumavati
Others Tara Devi

Mantra:

� ����� ������ ���

� JULY 2026 – SHAKTI OF EMOTIONAL CONTROL

Presiding Energy: *Bhuvaneshwari*

Birth Star Group	Shakti
Moon-ruled Nakshatras	Bhuvaneshwari
Others	Durga

Mantra:

� ����� ������������ ���

� AUGUST 2026 – SHAKTI OF POWER & AUTHORITY

Presiding Energy: *Mahakali / Pratyangira*

Birth Star	Shakti
Magha – Jyeshtha – Dhanishta	Pratyangira
Others	Mahakali

Mantra:

� ������� ������������� ���

� SEPTEMBER 2026 – SHAKTI OF BALANCE

Presiding Energy: *Durga / Annapurna*

Birth Star	Shakti
Virgo-Libra zone stars	Annapurna
Others	Durga

Mantra:

� ������������ ���

� OCTOBER 2026 – NAVARATRI MASTER MONTH

Presiding Energy: *All Nine Durgas*

Birth Star	Puja
All Nakshatras	Navadurga Puja (9 nights)

Mandatory Month for Everyone

� NOVEMBER 2026 – SHAKTI OF CONSOLIDATION

Presiding Energy: *Lakshmi*

Birth Star	Shakti
Rohini – Uttara – Hasta – Revati	Lakshmi
Others	Durga-Lakshmi combined

Mantra:

� ����� ������������ ���

� DECEMBER 2026 – SHAKTI OF CLOSURE & RELEASE

Presiding Energy: *Kali / Tara*

Birth Star Group	Shakti
End-cycle Nakshatras (Moola, Revati, Bhadra)	Kali
Others	Tara

Mantra:

� ����� �������� ���

� GENERAL RULES (IMPORTANT)

- Perform puja on Janma Nakshatra day of the month
- Avoid Rahu Kalam
- Prefer evening / Pradosha

- Simple offerings suffice: lamp, red flower, incense
- Consistency > complexity

◈ AUTHORIAL NOTE

"Shakti Puja is not ritual excess.

It is monthly psychological alignment with cosmic force."

PART 9 - CONCLUSION

(The Meaning of Time in 2026)

This section serves as the philosophical, spiritual, and practical closure of the entire 2026 Panchanga (Lahiri–Nirayana), written in formal English, faithful to traditional intent.

9.1 Time as a Moral Force

In Panchanga wisdom, time is not neutral.

It is an **active moral force** that rewards alignment and corrects deviation.

The year **2026** stands as a period where:

- Discipline is tested
- Intentions are examined
- Outcomes follow effort with precision

Time does not punish arbitrarily; it **educates through consequence**.

9.2 The Governing Pattern of 2026

The combined planetary rhythm of 2026 reveals a clear structure:

- **Saturn** enforces accountability and karmic

settlement
- **Jupiter** provides guidance, wisdom, and ethical expansion
- **Rahu and Ketu** accelerate inner transformation
- **The Sun** restores authority and order
- **The Moon** refines emotional intelligence

Together, they create a year that **rewards sincerity over cleverness.**

9.3 The Role of Human Choice

Astrology does not deny free will.

It clarifies the **conditions under which free will operates effectively**.

In 2026:

- Rash decisions invite resistance
- Patient action invites stability
- Ethical conduct multiplies gains

Those who move with awareness find fewer obstacles, even in difficult periods.

9.4 Ritual as Psychological Discipline

Ritual observance in the Panchanga is not mere formality.

It is a **discipline of attention**, aligning the individual mind with cosmic rhythm.

- Fasting strengthens restraint
- Charity dissolves ego
- Worship centers intention

In 2026, such practices act as **stabilizers against uncertainty**.

9.5 A Year of Inner Authority

The deeper message of 2026 is not external success, but **inner authority**.

- Authority over impulse
- Authority over fear
- Authority over distraction

Those who cultivate this inner governance experience outer order as a natural consequence.

9.6 Closing Guidance

To navigate 2026 effectively:

- Respect time, not fear it
- Act deliberately, not impulsively
- Choose restraint over excess
- Align effort with auspicious timing
- Let ethics guide ambition

Time, when honored, becomes an ally.

FINAL WORD

The 2026 Panchanga is not merely a calendar.

It is a map of disciplined living, a reminder that harmony arises when human intention and cosmic order move together.

May this year bring:

- Clarity of purpose
- Strength of character
- Peace through alignment

THE END

Also by Dr.Narayanan Namboodiri

Astrology Remedies & Solutions
KAAL SARP DOSHA: Truth, Symptoms & Remedies

Astrology Research & Analysis
Nakshatra Life Guide
Nakshatrakālam 2026
2026 to 2126 Birth Star Wise Analysis

About the Author

Dr. Narayanan Namboodiri is a respected spiritual guide, researcher, and practitioner of traditional Vedic astrology and remedial science, known for his calm wisdom, disciplined approach, and deeply realistic understanding of mystical subjects. With years of dedicated study and lived experience in India's spiritual traditions, he has built a reputation for guiding people through difficult life phases with clarity, balance, and practical solutions—without fear, exaggeration, or superstition.

What distinguishes Dr. Narayanan Namboodiri is his ability to interpret complex astrological patterns in a way that feels both spiritually authentic and intellectually grounded. His work focuses on the real-life impact of planetary influences—especially Rahu–Ketu patterns, karmic pressure cycles, and subtle spiritual disturbances that often appear during challenging periods. Rather than presenting doshas as "doom," he teaches that every astrological condition carries a correction path, and that discipline, awareness, and the right remedies can transform pressure into progress.

His writing style is clear, investigative, and structured. He approaches astrology as a science of patterns and consequences, explaining why certain struggles repeat, how specific planetary combinations influence decision-making, and what practical steps can reduce negativity and strengthen protection. His guidance is valued for being direct, usable, and deeply reassuring—offering readers not just information, but a stable mindset to face life with confidence.

Through his work in the **Astrology Reseach & Analysis** series, Dr. Narayanan Namboodiri continues to make traditional knowledge accessible to modern readers. His mission is to help individuals understand destiny without fear, correct karmic imbalances with sincerity, and develop spiritual strength through realistic remedial methods and inner transformation.

www.ingramcontent.com/pod-product-compliance
Lightning Source LLC
LaVergne TN
LVHW090404210926
848480LV00002B/437